Kensington PALACE

Kensington
PALACE

The OFFICIAL *Illustrated* HISTORY

EDWARD IMPEY

HISTORIC ROYAL PALACES

in association with

LONDON · NEW YORK

Kensington PALACE

The OFFICIAL *Illustrated* HISTORY

CONTENTS

Introduction

KENSINGTON PALACE is best known today as the former home of Diana, Princess of Wales, but it has been a royal residence for more than three centuries. The first house on the site, built in about 1620 by a London merchant, was one of several put up near the small village of Kensington to take advantage of the area's clean air and proximity to London. It was these qualities that were to shape Kensington's future: in 1689 William III and Mary II, needing somewhere more agreeable than the damp and smoky palace of Whitehall to attend to London business, bought the property and ordered Christopher Wren to enlarge it for their use. Thereafter, although much altered and enlarged, it remained, by royal standards, an unpretentious home. In this lies much of its appeal today: a group of buildings, at best semi-formal in design, in reddish-grey brick, surrounded by shrubberies and overlooking but in no way dominating the vast expanse of Kensington Gardens and Hyde Park. In its modesty also lies much of its historical interest, for its story sheds light on aspects and incidents of royal life and introduces us to royal personalities that would otherwise remain obscure. Kensington Palace is, however, a major national monument, shaped and decorated by the hands of some of the country's greatest architects, artists, craftsmen and designers, under the direction of several of its most cultivated rulers. A favoured residence of five sovereigns, it was the scene of many great events in the history of England and its ruling dynasties and, when the monarch was living there, the centre of its government.

This book tells the story of the site from before its acquisition by the Crown to the present day. It sets out the complex story of its architectural and decorative development, its surroundings and service buildings, and the creation and enhancement of Kensington's magnificent gardens. Intertwined with this is the story of political events that shaped the age, the way in which the palace was used, the people who lived there and their cultural and artistic interests, and the character and function of court life and ceremony. The later chapters, taking up the story after 1760, the last year of occupation by a reigning monarch, chronicle its fortunes as a residence for other members of the royal family; the birth and childhood of Queen Victoria, schemes for the palace's replacement or destruction, and the triumphant opening of the State Apartments to the public in 1898. The final chapters recount, among much else, the palace's temporary occupation by the London Museum, the conservation and presentation of the State Apartments and the installation and display of the world-renowned Royal Ceremonial Dress Collection.

TABLE OF OWNERSHIP

1605–20	House built and owned by Sir George Coppin
1620	Inherited by Robert Coppin, Sir George's brother
1629	Inherited by Thomas Coppin, Robert Coppin's son
1630–31	Bought by Sir Heneage Finch I
1631–61	Inhabited by Sir Heneage I's widow
1661	Inherited by Sir Heneage I's son, Sir John Finch, and sold to his brother, Sir Heneage II
1661–82	Owned and occupied by Sir Heneage Finch II, created 1st Earl of Nottingham in 1682
1682–89	Owned and occupied by Daniel Finch, 2nd Earl of Nottingham
1689	Bought by William III and Mary II, thus passing into royal ownership
1702–14	Queen Anne
1714–27	George I
1727–60	George II*
1760–1820	George III
1820–30	George IV
1830–37	William IV
1837–1901	Victoria
1901–10	Edward VII
1910–36	George V
1936	Edward VIII
1936–52	George VI
1952–	Elizabeth II

*George II was the last reigning monarch to inhabit Kensington Palace, but Queen Victoria lived there as a child.

2. *The Queen's Gallery as depicted by James Stephanoff and published in W.H. Pyne's* History of the Royal Residences *in 1819. The walls were hung with fabric by Mary II, but in George I's time were panelled and then painted white under Queen Caroline, who also hung the pictures as shown here. The medal cabinets to the right were placed there during the reign of George III.*

porc'. 7 l. ii. den'. In totis ualent' ual'. xx. lib. Xdo recep'.
simit' 7 sep. Hoc ad tenuit Wluuene ho regis. E. potuit
uende cui uoluit.

XXI. TERRA ALBERICI DE VER. OSVLVESTANE HVND.

ALBERICUS de uer' ten de epo constantiensi CHENESITT.
p. x. hid' se defd'. Tra e. x. car'. Ibi in dnio sunt. iiii. car.
7 uilli hnt. v. car'. 7 vi. pot' fieri. Ibi. xii. uilli. qsq; i. uirg.
7 vi. uilli de. iii. uirg'. ptr dim uirg'. 7 vii. serui. ptu. ii.
car'. pasta ad pecun uille. Silua. cc. porc' 7 iii. arpenn'
uinee. In totis ualent' ual'. x. lib. Xdo recep'. vi. lib. T.R.E.
x. lib. Hoc ad tenuit Eduuin' tegn regis. E. 7 uende potuit.

XXII. TERRA RADVLFI FRIS ILGERII. OSVLVESTANE HVND.

RADVLF' fr' Ilgerii. ten de rege TOLENTONE. p. ii. hid.
tra. e. ii. car'. In dnio. i. hid. 7 ibi. e. i. car'. Uilli hnt. ii. car.
Ibi. v. uilli qsq; de dim uirg'. 7 ii. bord. de xx. ac. 7 i. cot
7 i. seruus. pasta ad pec uille. Silua. lx. porc'. 7 v. solid.
H tra ual. xl. sol. Xdo recep'. lx. sol. T.R.E. xl. sol. hanc
tenuit Eduuin' ho regis. E. 7 uende potuit.

XXIII. TERRA PERMAN LVNDON. OSVLVESTANE HVND.

PERMAN ten de rege in Iseldone dim' hid. tra. e dim' car'.
Ibi. e un' uilts. h tra ual 7 ualuit. x. sol. hanc tra te
nuit Algar ho regis. E. 7 uende 7 dare potuit.

XXIIII. TERRA IVDITE COMITISSE. DELAELONE HVND.

IVDITA comitissa ten Tordtian de rege. p. v. hid se defd'
tra. e. x. car'. In dnio sunt caruciate que pt has v. hid.
7 ibi sunt. ii. car'. Uilli hnt. xii. car. ptr ht dim hid. 7 vi.
uilti de. vi. uirg' 7 xciiii. uilti qsq; de dim uirg'. 7 xii. bord.
qsq; de v. ac. 7 xcii. cot. Ibi. ii. francig' de. i. hid 7 iii. uirg.

KENSINGTON *before the*
PALACE

Kensington appears in the Domesday Book and passes through successive aristocratic and monastic owners. The first house on the site, later the nucleus of the royal palace, is built by George Coppin; it becomes the home of the Earl of Nottingham, a politician much involved in the Glorious Revolution of 1688 that sweeps William III and Mary II to the throne in 1689.

The Middle Ages

The manor of Kensington is listed in the Domesday Book, the great survey of English property compiled for William the Conqueror in 1086, as are the neighbouring manors of Chelsea, Fulham and 'Eia'. From this we learn that Kensington had been held before 1066 by a certain Edwin, a thegn (a minor landholder in the service of a greater one), of whom nothing else is known. Its new holder was Aubrey de Vere, whose family had come from Vair (near Nantes in Brittany) and who was himself the feudal tenant of Geoffrey of Montbray, Bishop of Coutances. Created Earls of Oxford in 1155, the de Veres were to become one of the great families of England and to retain links with Kensington until the reign of Henry VIII (1509–47). The Domesday property, extending over about 1500 acres and valued at £10 per year, included wood for 200 pigs, pasture, plough land and a *vinea* (probably a vineyard). It also included land to support a priest and must, therefore, have had a church, which can be presumed to have been where St Mary's church is today and to have served a small settlement. Bordering it to the east was the manor of 'Eia', which by 1100 had been divided into three parts, one of which retained the original name, soon recast as 'Hyde'; this extended over about 900 acres between the two streams that ran across what is now Hyde Park: the Tyburn, and the stream to the west of it called the West Bourne.

Within a generation of 1086 the Domesday manor of Kensington was, like that of Hyde, fragmented, creating boundaries still evident in today's topography that framed the surroundings of the future palace. The process began when Aubrey de Vere's son, Geoffrey, grateful for the attentions of Faritius, Abbot of the great abbey at Abingdon (on the Thames, a few miles upstream from Oxford), petitioned his father to grant to the abbey a portion of the manor and the right to appoint the parish priest. This then became a manor in its own right, called the Abbots' Manor, and covered about 270 acres between what is now Church Street and the western boundary of the manor of Hyde, later that of

the park. The church took on the name of St Mary Abbots', and a long strip of land, extending (according to today's topography) from Vicarage Gate to the Bayswater Road and east–west between Brunswick Gardens and Palace Gardens Terrace, was soon set aside to support its incumbent. The remaining land was then referred to as the Earls' Manor – commemorated today in the name Earls Court.

In the thirteenth century a portion of land still further west, although retained by the earls, became another separate or subsidiary manor by the name of West Town, and in the next century the portion of the Domesday manor to the south of what is now Kensington High Street passed out of the family through marriage. The parts left to the de Veres – West Town and an area to the north of (what is now) the Bayswater Road, known as Notting Barns or Notting Hill – were temporarily lost to them after 1461, when they found themselves on the losing Lancastrian side in the first of the 'Wars of the Roses'. Although later restored to them under Henry VII (1485–1509), Notting Barns was sold in 1488, soon coming into the hands of the monks of Westminster who, since about 1100, were also the owners of the manor of Hyde. The de Veres' last property at Kensington, West Town, passed to other noble families in 1526.

The creation of the house and its estate

Walter Cope and the assembly of the Kensington estate
In 1536 Henry VIII obtained the manor of Hyde from the abbey of Westminster in exchange for a former monastic estate in Berkshire, and enclosed over 600 acres of it as a deer park. Its northern boundary, as today, was marked by the Bayswater Road – then called Acton Road – and its southern limit by a road on the approximate course of Kensington High Street. With the dissolution of Abingdon Abbey in 1538, the monastic portions of Kensington also became Crown property and remained so until towards the end of the century, when the de Veres' former estate was briefly reassembled in private hands.

The reassembly process began with the activities of a certain Sir Walter Cope, who was born in the

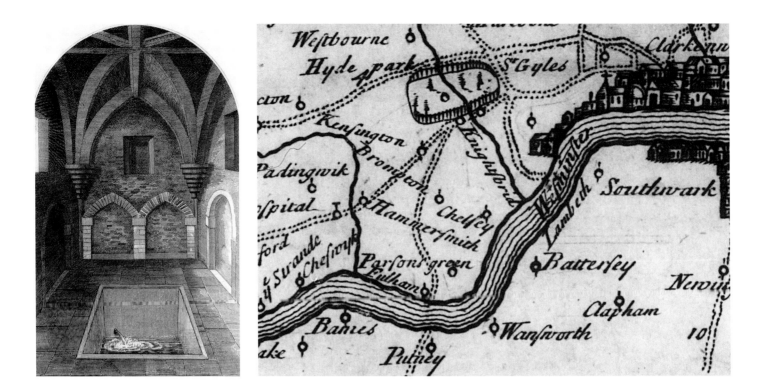

ABOVE LEFT 4. *Interior of the 'Conduit House' built for Henry VIII, which stood until 1871 to the south-west of the palace. It was built to protect a spring, from where water was piped southwards to the manor house at Chelsea that Henry had acquired in 1536.*

ABOVE RIGHT 5. *Detail from an early eighteenth-century edition of John Norden's* Survey of Middlesex, *dating from 1593. The site of the future palace and its grounds lay immediately to the west (left) of the 'pale' or fence and ditch surrounding Hyde Park, created by Henry VIII in 1536. The east–west road to the north is now the Bayswater Road, and that to the south is roughly on the line of Kensington High Street.*

1550s, the younger son of a minor Oxfordshire family. Nothing is known of his early career, but by the 1590s he was in the service of Robert Cecil, 1st Earl of Salisbury and Chief Minister successively to Elizabeth I (1558–1603) and James I (1603–25). Under Cecil's enviable patronage, Cope was appointed to a string of lucrative and influential posts, becoming joint Keeper of Hyde Park and Chamberlain of the Exchequer, and sitting in a succession of parliaments. In 1603, already a man of substance, he was knighted by the new king. Much of Cope's new wealth went into land purchases, concentrated in Kensington: his first, in 1591, was the manor and estate of West Town, followed in 1599 by the Abbots' Manor and Notting Barns, which he sold off in the following year. His choice may have been influenced by his keepership of the adjoining park, perhaps also by the proximity of Cecil's own suburban house on the river at Chelsea (fig. 22), but undoubtedly by Kensington's position both in open country and close to London. This was important, as Cope's intention was to provide himself with a residence surrounded by enough land to uphold his status and ensure his privacy but within a short distance of Whitehall, where much of his business and official work was conducted. In doing so he was following a fashion that had begun in the last years of Elizabeth I's reign and become established under James I, as the court became less peripatetic and the work of lawyers and government expanded.

This social phenomenon also had an architectural response in the type of house that came to be known as the 'villa'. Anticipated in the design of the small

but lavishly equipped 'lodges', in which great men provided temporary accommodation on extended hunting trips, such houses had all the recognizable elements of a grand house, but quite differently arranged: a 'double-pile' plan (two rooms thick) allowed for an abandonment of the traditional linear arrangement of rooms and for more complicated communication between them. Surviving examples include Eagle House, Wimbledon (1613), and the so-called 'Dutch House' in Kew Gardens, built for a London merchant in about 1630 (fig. 8). Cope's house was one of three important and pioneering examples built at Kensington in the early seventeenth century, the other two being Campden House and its smaller neighbour, later called Nottingham House, which was bought by William III (1689–1702) and Mary II (1689–94) in 1689. The earliest of these, and perhaps the most innovative in layout, was Campden House, known from early views (fig. 6), which survived, although much altered, until it burnt down in 1862. A plan of it, more or less as built, is contained among the 150 drawings of contemporary houses made by the land-surveyor and antiquary John Thorpe (c. 1565–1655); he also included an alternative scheme, which suggests that this may have been one of the rare ones he designed himself. The former existence of the building is today commemorated in a number of street names.

Completed by about 1605, the house may have first been used by Cope himself, who had been deprived of the old manor house of Abbots' Manor following a lawsuit with his main tenant, Robert Horseman, in 1599. It was soon sold, however, to a

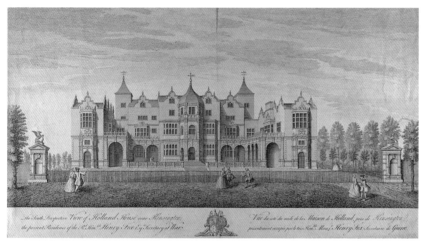

TOP 6. *View of the south front of Campden House in 1795 by the architect and antiquarian William Capon. Built c. 1605, this was the first of the three 'villas' that dominated Kensington for the next century and, like Holland House, was used, although never owned, by the royal family.*

MIDDLE 7. *A view of Holland House from the south in 1751. This was built for Sir Walter Cope in 1606–14 to a design at least improved by John Thorpe; its construction firmly established Kensington as a fashionable suburb and encouraged the building of its neighbour to the east, eventually to become the nucleus of Kensington Palace.*

BOTTOM 8. *The house built at Kew in about 1630 for a London merchant, now known either as the Dutch House or, thanks to its use by the royal family from 1728 until 1818, Kew Palace. Although less sophisticated than Sir George Coppin's house at Kensington, Kew is an important representative of the villa type. The original pink colouring was reinstated by Historic Royal Palaces in 1997.*

rich merchant and Gloucestershire landowner, Baptist Hicks, later Viscount Campden of Chipping Campden, from which the house took its name. In any case, from 1606 Cope was building a new house nearby, probably not at first to Thorpe's design, although Thorpe was responsible for alterations to it in 1612 when work was still in progress. The house was popularly known in Cope's lifetime as 'Cope's Castle', presumably on account of its turreted roofline and commanding position, but not, perhaps, without a touch of ridicule. It was later named Holland House after the title bestowed on his heir and son-in-law, Richard Rich, 1st Earl of Holland (named after, but not associated with, Holland in Lincolnshire). As its early name suggests, it was a big and splendid house, later to be used as a temporary residence by William and Mary, and survived intact until largely destroyed by enemy action in 1941. Having overreached himself, however, Cope had been selling off sections of his Kensington property, including, at some stage before his death in 1614, a plot between Church Street and Hyde Park, eventually to become the site and grounds of the royal palace.

George Coppin and his house at Kensington

The purchaser of Cope's property was Sir George Coppin who, like Cope, was a businessman, politician, minor landowner and servant of Robert Cecil, and who had been knighted in the same year. The two men certainly knew each other, and their acquaintance, together with Kensington's newly fashionable status, probably explains his choice. In the middle of

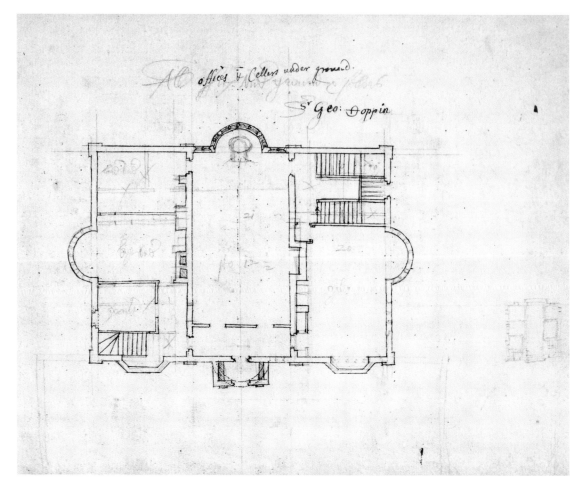

9. Plan of Sir George Coppin's house by John Thorpe, included in his manuscript compilation called the Book of Architecture. *That this represents the house at Kensington, later to become the nucleus of the palace, is clear from plans made after 1689 in which the outline of the early house can be made out (figs. 10, 47).*

his new property Coppin then built the house, on a fresh site, which was later bought by King William. The building itself is known from a sketch plan by John Thorpe (fig. 9), identified as Coppin's by the annotation of his name in Thorpe's hand, and shown to be the house at Kensington by its appearance, at the core of Kensington House, in Wren's plans of 1689 and later (figs. 10, 47); whether it was Thorpe's own design remains, unfortunately, unknown. Usually dated to 1605, its construction was probably rather later, although it could have been put up at any stage between Coppin's purchase of the site and his death in 1620. It is referred to in his will as "lately built" and, as his widow never moved there, may not have been finished even by then.

In addition to its importance as the future nucleus of a royal palace, Coppin's house was of considerable architectural and historical interest as an early 'villa'. Although smaller than either Holland or Campden House, and in some ways less advanced, it was still very ingenious and perfect (fig. 9). Here, the largest room was still the hall, but in this case placed not on the building's longer axis, in the medieval tradition of the 'great hall', but across it, which allowed for a symmetrical plan. This arrangement, known as the 'through hall', is first recorded at Holdenby Lodge, on Christopher Hatton's great Northamptonshire estate,

and survives at Hardwick Hall in Derbyshire, built in 1592. In plan and appearance Coppin's house was an elaborate structure, with bay windows on all elevations, the one to the north lighting the hall at ground-floor level and the main room above. The only view of the original building dates from about 1689, after its partial concealment by Wren's additions, but clearly shows part of its north front, crowned by elaborate 'Dutch' gables and the (mutilated) bow window of the hall (fig. 23). Based on this, on what can be deduced from the plan and inferred from comparable structures, and aided by Patrick Faulkner's clever reconstruction, fig. 28 probably gives a fair impression of the building's appearance. Its original internal arrangement, beyond the layout of the rooms on the main floor, the position of the hall and the Great Chamber immediately above, and the raising of the whole house over a basement containing kitchens and service rooms, cannot be reconstructed. The first real information beyond Thorpe's plan, in the form of an inventory, dates from 1662, by which time it had probably been enlarged. The house was certainly surrounded by gardens, but, again, nothing is known of their layout.

At Sir George Coppin's death in 1620 the house passed to his brother, Robert. He died in 1629, leaving it to his son, Thomas; from him it passed to the Finch family, who held it for three generations until its sale to William III in 1689.

The Finches at Kensington

Heneage Finch I

Born in 1580 and named after his mother's family, Heneage Finch had had a distinguished career as a lawyer and politician by the 1620s, and was knighted in 1623, but had no house of his own conveniently near Westminster. The dowry received on his second marriage, in 1627, may have encouraged him to find one; in any case, in or around 1630 he bought the Coppin property, as is shown by the reference in his will of 1631 to "my dwellinge house near Kensington with the gardens and grounds thereto adjoining and all the other lands which I lately bought of ... Mr Coppin". Whether he altered or even used the house is unclear, but his widow lived there until her death in 1661.

The country, meanwhile, had been convulsed by the Civil War. Although there was no fighting at Kensington, the war came quite close in the form of the earthwork defences thrown up by Parliament in 1643 at the far (east) end of the park, which later gave

their name to Mount Street in Mayfair. From the end of the war in 1649 until the Restoration in 1660, the country was governed first by Parliament and then as a virtual dictatorship under the Lord Protector, Oliver Cromwell. Although the Finches came through the war and the 'Interregnum' unscathed, the sale of royal property that followed the execution of Charles I had some local impact as it was intended to include Hyde Park. Certainly, the commercial development of the two lots touching its western boundary, within 30 m (100 ft) of the Finch property, could have had a major impact on its environment and thus on its future. In the event, however, the purchasers made little use of their investment and lost it following the restoration of the monarchy in 1660, although the eastern boundary of the property seems to have remained a feature of the landscape until the eighteenth century.

Heneage Finch II, 1st Earl of Nottingham

In 1661 the Kensington property passed to Heneage's younger son, Sir John Finch, a doctor and diplomat who had served at the court of the Grand Duke of Tuscany in Florence and at the Ottoman court in

10. *Plan of Kensington House of 1696–99, after major additions by William III, clearly showing the early seventeenth-century house embedded within it, its original floor plan still more or less intact. Particularly distinctive are the bow windows to the north (top) and west.*

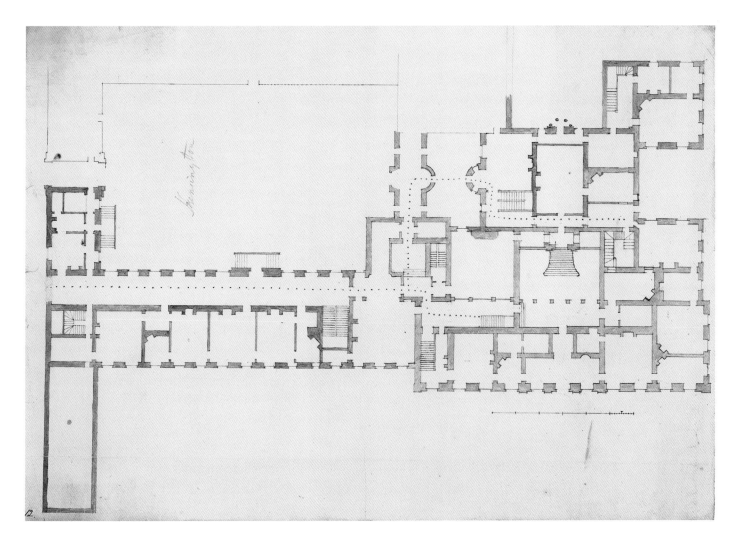

Constantinople. Having no use for the house, but presumably wishing to keep it in the family, he sold it for £2500 to his brother, named Heneage after their father. Another gifted lawyer, and one of the leading royalist spokesmen in the Convention Parliament which worked towards the Restoration of 1660, Heneage was soon favoured by the new regime: in that same year he was knighted; he became Solicitor-General in 1670, Lord Keeper of the Great Seal in 1673, Lord Chancellor and Baron Finch of Daventry in 1674; and in 1681 he was created Earl of Nottingham.

Documents associated with Sir Heneage's purchase provide some useful information about the property, the purchase agreement stating that it included "all those houses, edifices, buildings, barnes, stables, outhouses, gardens, orchards ... and all hangings, furniture and moveables within the building". The property attached to the house evidently remained that purchased from Coppin, largely contained by the "fences and pales" of Hyde Park to the east, by the glebe of St Mary's to the west and by the roads to the north and south. The land itself was put to a variety of uses, including pasture, woodland and arable (although some lay in separate parcels), a reminder of the essentially rural rather than suburban nature of the surroundings.

Anticipating the eastward extension of the grounds of the next century, Sir Heneage soon acquired from the King a strip of land 6 m (20 ft) wide, stretching the full length of his property between the two roads; the Royal Warrant describes this as "all that ditch and fence which divides our park from the grounds of the said Sir Heneage Finch ... and also all the trees therein growing and ... ten foot in breadth and 150 rodds in length of the soyle of Hyde Park beyond the said fence". As the park boundary, running within 30 m (100 ft) of his house, was by now completely overgrown, the purchase was probably intended to open up its eastward view.

Of the gardens and surroundings of the house we have no plans or pictures, but features within them and their attractiveness are referred to by various visitors. Inevitably these include Samuel Pepys: on a visit in 1664 to see his superior at the Admiralty, Edward Montagu, who was lodged nearby, Pepys wandered in: "going into Sir Finch's garden" he enjoyed "the fountayne and singing there with the ladies", remarking on what "a mighty fine cool place it is, with a great laver of water in the middle, and the bravest place for music I ever heard". A particularly attractive part of the garden, or at least one favoured by Pepys, had been created in the plot in the southwest corner of the main property, in the area later occupied by the royal kitchen gardens (fig. 107). Known as the 'More', thanks to its former description as a marsh or 'mere', since the 1530s this had been the site of a 'conduit head', which by 1662 had been joined by a decorative 'marble conduit' and was adjacent to a 'grotto' – probably a mock cave, of the type made fashionable earlier in the century by the French designer Isaac de Caus. This was where Pepys and his inevitable lady friends, on another visit, "sang to my great content", although the ambience was briefly dented by seeing one of Finch's sons beat a dog to death in front of them. In all probability, however, the main gardens lay directly to the north and south of the house, overlooked by its best rooms.

A key asset of the house was what Elizabeth Finch described in a letter to her husband as the "fresh air you have att Kensington" – a quality that was to have a vital bearing on its future. Its situation also made its roof a good vantage point over the city, from which Finch enjoyed one of the lesser-known viewings of the Great Fire of London. Afterwards he wrote in a private letter:

> Had your Lordship been at Kensington, you would have thought for five days together, for so long the Fire lasted, it had been Domesday and that the heavens themselves had been on fire, and the fearfull cryes and howlings of undone people

11. Samuel Pepys, whose diaries of 1660–69 are such a valuable source of information and anecdote about London life. Pepys visited Kensington on many occasions in the 1660s and left useful impressions of Finch's gardens. Portrait by John Hayls, 1666.

main house – some, for example, being in the "Cook's room in the clock house" or the "garden house by Acton [Bayswater] road". The main house, however, clearly contained at least thirty rooms, which cannot all have lain within Coppin's original house, so the Finches must have substantially enlarged it. Although the date, form and site of these additions are unknown, they may have comprised a new wing extending northwards on the site of the existing Queen's Apartments, which clearly incorporate earlier work (see below). In the meantime, the interior of the old house had itself undergone some structural alteration, as is shown, for example, by reference to the porter's chamber under the "new great stairs", although whether these were a rebuild of those shown by Thorpe (fig. 9) is unknown.

Daniel Finch, 2nd Earl of Nottingham

On the death of the 1st Earl of Nottingham in 1683, his Kensington house, by now – thanks to the tradition of naming noblemen's houses after their titles – known as Nottingham House, passed to his eldest son, Daniel. Already a well-established lawyer, Daniel Finch had also begun a long career in government service under Charles II (1660–85), having served as an MP in the parliament of 1673–79, on the Admiralty Commission from April 1679 and as a Privy Councillor from 1680. Under James II (1685–88) and William III (1689–1702) he continued in high office, and was involved in politics at the highest level (see below) into the reigns of Queen Anne (1702–14) and George I (1714–27). His appearance, however, seems to have invited as much comment as his talents, Mary II (1689–94) later remarking on his "grave look" and a satirical article of 1709 calling him "Don Diego Dismallo" – a nickname that Jonathan Swift and others attributed to his "spanish" colouring and "solemn countenance" (fig. 12). Whether he made any improvements to the house or its gardens is unknown, but his correspondence identifies Kensington as his main residence, shared with his wife and two children, and after 1685 with his second wife, Anne Hatton, with whom he was to have twenty more. As his family grew, however, Nottingham House must have become increasingly cramped, a factor that added to Finch's readiness to sell it to King William in 1689.

The Glorious Revolution

By the time Daniel Finch succeeded to the earldom in 1683, events were under way that would lead, a few years later, to the flight of James II and his replacement by William III and Mary II as joint sovereigns. The impact on Kensington of this gigantic political upheaval, known as the 'Glorious Revolution', was that it became royal property, but it was also associated, through Daniel Finch's involvement, with the progress of events themselves.

12. *Daniel Finch, 2nd Earl of Nottingham, attributed to Jonathan Richardson, 1726. It was from Finch, a distinguished politician heavily involved in the events that brought them to the throne, that William and Mary bought Nottingham House in 1689.*

did much encrease the resemblance. My walkes and Gardens were almost covered with the ashes of papers, linens … and pieces of ceeling and plaster work blown hither by the Tempest.

A 1664 inventory of all Sir Heneage's moveable property shows that he lived in some style, as befitted his rising fortunes and position. Another of 1676, by which time he had been made Lord Chancellor and created 1st Baron Daventry, shows that his house was lavishly furnished and rich in exotic textiles and upholstery – by far the most expensive components. His Lordship's bedroom, for example, contained four pieces of tapestry, crimson damask curtains and valance, a counterpane and carpet, two 'Turkey work' carpets, a large 'Persian' carpet, six chairs and three low stools, four window curtains of crimson taffeta, and a feather bed and bedding. The appearance of the interiors must have resembled those that survive to this day at Ham House, near Richmond in Surrey, a house of similar scale furnished in the 1670s for John Maitland, Lord Lauderdale, Finch's colleague in royal service. Not all the material listed was found in the

13. Bed made in about 1685, almost certainly installed by Daniel Finch at Nottingham House and subsequently moved to Burley-on-the-Hill in Rutland, the main seat of the family from the 1690s. In 1974 it was bought for the Dutch palace of Het Loo – as it happened, one of the former residences of William and Mary – and is shown here displayed in the bedchamber Mary used as Princess of Orange.

In 1685 Charles II had been succeeded by his brother, James, Duke of York, in spite of repeated attempts by Parliament to pass a Bill of Exclusion to disqualify him on the grounds of his Catholic faith. Meanwhile, in 1677 James's eldest daughter, Mary, a Protestant, had married William, the ruler or 'Stadtholder' of the United Netherlands – nominally an elected post, but one that had been his father's and was made hereditary in 1674. William owed his title of Prince of Orange to his family's possession of the town and principality of Orange in the south of France, until these were seized by Louis XIV in 1672.

As things stood in England in 1685, Mary was the undisputed heir to the throne, and William was content to keep a close eye on English politics, to encourage James to ally with him against the French, and to wait.

In spite of James's early promises not to promote Catholics to high office, his blatant disregard for this agreement alienated even the Tories – the parliamentary group recently formed in opposition to his 'exclusion', and who were usually his natural supporters. As early as September 1686 the King's Catholicizing programme led Lord Mordaunt, leader of the Tories' parliamentary opponents, the Whigs, to invite the Stadtholder to invade. William refused, but in the following year he sent emissaries for secret discussions with prominent politicians, including Lord Nottingham, to assess the likely level of support he would receive, should intervention be needed. For the moment, though, there was still no urgency, for Mary remained the heir, James was already in his mid-fifties, and his second wife, Mary Beatrice of Modena, had had six children who died in infancy and was now considered unlikely to have any more.

The situation, however, changed dramatically in September 1687 with the Queen's pregnancy. William now expressed to his correspondents of the previous year a willingness, as Nottingham later put it, "to come to relieve England from its fears" if formally invited to do so. Nottingham himself, though, unwilling to break his oath to James, pulled out, alarming his co-conspirators to the extent that they considered his assassination. In 1688 the pace of events was again accelerated, first by James's Declaration of Indulgence, permitting public worship by Catholics and 'Dissenters' (non-Anglican Protestants), and secondly by the Queen's delivery in June of a son. Although Protestant cynics suggested the baby had been smuggled in in a warming-pan, his legitimacy was not seriously in doubt and was later confirmed by the painter Sir Godfrey Kneller, whose knowledge of royal physiognomy was second to none. In any case, now faced with the immediate risk of a Catholic succession and in no doubt of the King's religious policy, the 'Immortal Seven' peers drafted a letter on 30 June formally inviting William's intervention. This time he accepted, although his declared intention was described as not "to dethrone the King or to conquer England, but only to ensure that by a convocation of a free parliament ... the reformed religion will be secure and out of danger". In July and August, secure in the knowledge that Louis XIV's armies were tied up far from Holland's borders, William mobilized his forces for the descent on England.

At last realizing the danger he was in, James reversed his Catholicizing programme, offered a range of political concessions and put his substantial standing army and navy on the alert. But he was too late. After a false start, William's warships and transports sailed on 10 November, bypassed James's fleet off the Essex coast and – William's choice being dictated by the wind – landed at Brixham in Devon on 5 December. There he met no resistance and marched inland, gathering support as James's wavering troops fell back before him. In desperation, on 18 December James sent a deputation of three loyal ministers – the Marquess of Halifax, Sidney Godolphin and the Earl of Nottingham – to meet the Prince, and peaceful measures for achieving William's aims by means of a free parliament were sincerely discussed. But James, while the chance to retain the throne lay within his grasp, chose this moment to flee to France, destroying the loyalty of his most

14. *The departure of the Dutch fleet from Holland in November 1688, as imagined by the artist and engraver Daniel Marot. Although William was fully equipped to fight at sea and on land, his intention at this stage was simply to safeguard England from Catholicism and the French, and to secure the succession of Mary, James II's daughter.*

Vertrek van zyn Koninglyke Hooghaid van Hellevoetsluis na Engeland.

23
QUEEN MARY.   WISSING.

15. *Mary II when Princess of Orange, by Willem Wissing, c. 1685. This was probably the portrait painted, at the command of James II, when the artist was sent to Holland in 1685.*

faithful supporters; as London threatened to descend into anarchy, William had little choice but to accept the leadership of a provisional government.

The first task for the new leader was to assemble a parliament – or, as it was called by William, "a Convention" – which met in January 1689. The most immediate question was who would wear the crown: William alone (as he wished), Mary alone (as the Tories wished, but she did not) or Mary as 'regent' on James's behalf, as suggested by Lord Nottingham? It became apparent that joint rule was the only solution – satisfying William and respecting the legitimacy of Mary's claim – and they were formally offered the Crown on 13 February, as William III and Mary II, in a ceremony at the Banqueting House, Whitehall. There they learned of and accepted the many clauses of the Declaration of Rights, among which were the provisions that Mary's sister, Anne, would succeed if Mary had no children, and that no Catholic could ever become king or queen of England.

16. *William III by Sir Godfrey Kneller, 1701. This portrait, which hangs in the King's Presence Chamber at Hampton Court, was commissioned in 1700 to commemorate William's contribution to the Treaty of Ryswick of 1696, by which Louis XIV had renounced further territorial ambitions in Europe and recognized William, rather than James II, as King of Great Britain. Intended to glorify the King's statesmanship and martial prowess, it shows him partly in seventeenth-century dress and armour, but with the boots and bare legs of a Roman emperor, and receiving the adulation of various Classical deities.*

The Royal Residence:
KENSINGTON under WILLIAM and MARY 1689–1702

Disliking their most important London residence, Whitehall Palace, the new sovereigns seek a new home nearby and purchase Nottingham House. Sir Christopher Wren enlarges it to suit the needs and formalities of court life; the house is furnished and becomes a lively royal home. Further additions are made to the building, and the first royal gardens are laid out.

LEFT 17. *The King's Great Bedchamber at Hampton Court, much as it looked in the last years of William's reign. Its equivalent at Kensington after 1689 was smaller and lower, and its decoration and furnishings were probably less ornate, but the room was presumably similar in its general effect.*

BELOW 18. *'Bird's-eye' view of Whitehall Palace from the east, drawn between 1695 and 1697 by Leonard Knyff. In the centre is the Banqueting House, built for James I by Inigo Jones; extending towards the viewer at the left are the royal apartments put up by Christopher Wren for James II. In the background is St James's Park, overlooked by St James's Palace (top centre). Kensington lies out of sight, two miles further east.*

The search for a new house

The royal houses in 1689

Immediately beset by constitutional and political issues, hostility abroad and the very real threat of Scottish resistance in support of James II, William and Mary had a great deal to occupy them in the first months of their reign. Of more personal but no less immediate urgency, however, was the question of where they would live. The vast number of houses kept in readiness for royal use in earlier reigns in the London area had dwindled to a mere handful, largely during the years after the Civil War. In the city, the once lavish accommodation at the Tower of London had been useless for a century, while the royal lodgings at the still more ancient Palace of Westminster had burnt down in 1512. Charles II had begun a magnificent palace at Greenwich but, tired of London, had transferred his resources to building a new one at Winchester, which his successor abandoned. Within London's immediate orbit the new sovereigns were left, therefore, with the vast, sprawling palace of Whitehall – largely the work of Henry VIII, although incorporating elements of the London house of the

archbishops of York – and St James's Palace, built on the site of a former leper hospital in the 1520s. Further afield, they inherited the old but magnificent palace at Hampton Court (see below) and, even more distant, the great castle at Windsor.

From Mary's arrival in England on 11 February 1689 until their formal acceptance of the Crown, William and Mary lodged at St James's, but thereafter were expected to live at Whitehall. The Stuart kings had added many fine buildings to the palace, including the Banqueting House (finished for James I in 1622) and the new royal apartments added by Charles II and James II (fig. 18), but it was far from ideal. Although away from the most populated areas, Whitehall was heavily polluted by their smoke, while the site, low lying and on the very edge of the Thames, was subject to flooding and damp. To William, who suffered from chronic and on occasion life-threatening asthma, this was a serious problem – one he acknowledged, writing from London, to be "getting worse in this climate, which makes me weak". In addition, residence at Whitehall required the observation of formalities of court life that the King wished to avoid as much as possible. An alternative residence in which they could be more comfortable had to be sought, although Whitehall would remain their formal London home.

Only nine days into their reign – prompted perhaps by Mary's childhood memories – the King and Queen visited Hampton Court, on the Thames beyond Kingston. Both immediately took a liking to it and, as a contemporary wrote, the King "found the air of Hampton Court agreed so well with him that he resolved to live the greatest part of the year there". William and Mary stayed there from the end of March until October 1689, partly in the old Tudor apartments, partly in those added by Charles II (fig. 19) and latterly in the Tudor 'Water Gallery', specially fitted up for Mary's use. Splendid as it was, however, the Tudor palace was now hopelessly old-fashioned, and after a series of still more ambitious schemes had been rejected, the creation of the royal apartments in their present form was under way by May 1689.

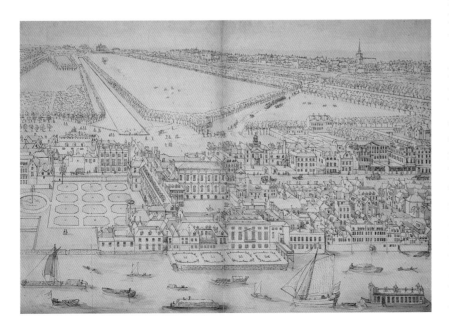

ABOVE 19. *View of Hampton Court Palace from the east, much as William and Mary encountered it in 1689. Taking an immediate liking to the palace, they made frequent use of it, particularly in the summer. At first they used the apartments added by Charles II (seen to the extreme left of the main buildings), but by May of 1689 the rebuilding of the royal apartments in their present form had already begun.*

RIGHT 20. *Leonard Knyff's 'bird's-eye' view of Hampton Court Palace from the east, painted in the first years of Queen Anne's reign (1702–14). The regular façades of the apartments rebuilt for William and Mary can be seen facing the great semi-circular Fountain Garden in the foreground. The contrast between the vast splendours of Hampton Court and the King's very modest house at Kensington was great, but entirely deliberate: they were not merely alternative residences, but served quite different purposes.*

Agreeable as Hampton Court may have been for the new sovereigns, its location, several hours from London, was a major problem for their officials. William's key minister, the Marquess of Halifax, complained that "the King's inaccessibleness and liveing so at Hampton Court altogether, and at as soe active a time ruined all business". But while in summer it was at least feasible for courtiers and ministers to leave the capital for Hampton Court, in winter this would have been almost impossible: not only would the journey have been more difficult but also this was the time, between November and April, when the business of parliament and the law courts required their presence in London. The obvious answer was to seek a house nearer the city, a move becoming more urgent as the parliamentary sessions at the end of the year approached, and "to please them", as Mary put it in her memoir for 1689, "the King bought Lord Nottingham's house at Kensington".

Nottingham House

Kensington probably came to the King's notice as he rode out into the country along what is now Kensington High Street, taking the preferred northerly route to Hampton Court via Hammersmith, Brentford and Twickenham. The most prominent house in the neighbourhood, Holland House, was the first to suggest itself as a possible residence, and the King inspected it early in 1689 but disliked it; its owner, Lord Holland, may also have been reluctant to part with it on a permanent basis. The King's actual choice of the much smaller Nottingham House was based on a mixture of its merits and its availability. Unlike Holland House, which stood on the edge of a slope, the Finches' house stood on a relatively flat site, which would have made its extension easier. Another factor was probably its situation on the edge of Hyde Park, which, as royal property, would have given the King and Queen control over the views to the east and allowed for any amount of extension to its grounds. In addition, the fact that the house could be reached from St James's by travelling across Hyde Park and St James's Park (the part now called Green Park) without using public roads, probably appealed to the King's desire for privacy; certainly it was an advantage he made use of, as he swiftly created a private road along the southern length of Hyde Park. This road, although re-routed during the reign of George II

(1727–60), survives as Rotten Row (possibly a corruption of *Route du Roi*, or 'the King's Road'; fig. 62). Meanwhile, the King was aware that Lord Nottingham, once again a Privy Councillor, had long been seeking a new base for his family and would be a willing vendor.

The deal with Nottingham must have been struck by mid-June 1689, as the house was then already being enlarged for the sovereigns' use, but the first instalment was not paid until July, "payment in full of £20,000 for the purchase of his Lordship's House, gardens and lands lying and being within the walls of Kensington in Middlesex" being made in March the following year. The Finches, meanwhile, remained in Nottingham House until September 1689, the King and Queen taking up residence from August to December at Holland House, partly to keep an eye on the work at their new house. Meanwhile, Mary's sister, Princess Anne, and her husband, Prince George, took a long lease of Campden House, which they kept on until Anne's own accession to the throne in 1702.

"Very noble, tho' not great": the creation of Kensington House, 1689–94

Sir Christopher Wren

The means by which Lord Nottingham's house was made suitable for royal use, probably the assurance that it could be done at all, and certainly its direction, were all the work of Sir Christopher Wren. Wren had begun his career as an astronomer and mathematician, becoming Savilian Professor of Astronomy at Oxford in 1661, but was soon encouraged to put his interest in architecture – a favoured accomplishment for gentlemen – into practice. Having caught the eye of Charles II, in 1667 he was appointed to the committee advising on the rebuilding of London after the

Great Fire. The next year saw him appointed as Surveyor-General of the King's Works, in charge of the Office of Works – the government department that built and maintained Crown buildings. But in spite of Wren's record, his continued service after 1689 was by no means automatic, for he was firmly identified with the previous regime and William might well have given the post to a Dutchman – as he did, for example, with the Superintendency of the Royal Gardens – or to someone who had been firmly on the right side in the recent crisis, unlike Wren, who had served as a Tory MP in 1685–87. But in the event Wren swiftly gained the confidence of the King and Queen – particularly, and probably decisively, that of Mary, who, as an Anglican of renewed enthusiasm, first encountered the architect thanks to her interest in the rebuilding of St Paul's Cathedral; as his son later wrote, the two were soon conversing freely on architectural subjects and mathematics, and later kept closely in touch as the various royal building works progressed. Wren's deputy as Comptroller of Works, however, was a more political appointment – the brilliant but difficult William Talman, a protégé of William's favourite, Hans Willem Bentinck, 1st Earl of Portland. More important for Kensington, however, was Nicholas Hawksmoor, who had worked with Wren since the mid-1680s as a draughtsman and later practised as an architect of brilliance in his own right. Wren's work at Kensington, although never spectacular or ranked among his greatest achievements, and today lacking all but fragments of its grandest parts, nevertheless displayed the ingenuity that was such a conspicuous part of his talent. In any case, it was his work in 1689 and his continued

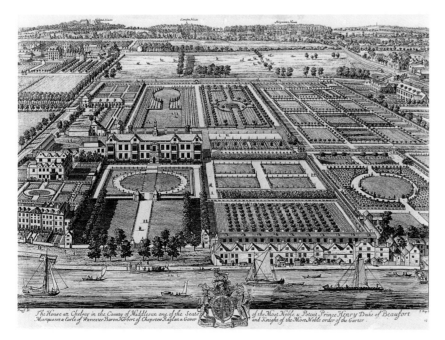

ABOVE LEFT 23. *The north side of Kensington House, as depicted by the draughtsman and engraver Sutton Nicholls between 1689 and 1694. At the centre can be seen part of the early seventeenth-century house, complete with its (mutilated) bow window and 'Dutch' gables; to either side are the 'pavilions' added for William and Mary in 1689. The central doorway is on the approximate site of the existing doorway into the Red Saloon.*

ABOVE RIGHT 24. *Painting of about 1700 by Adam Frans van der Meulen showing building work at Versailles. Although Kensington was on a far smaller scale, Wren's workmen there used similar tools and techniques. Note the scaffolding and hoist to the right and the group in the foreground discussing a plan of the new work.*

contribution throughout the remainder of William's reign, and during that of his successor, Queen Anne, which created the essentials of the building that we know today.

The first phase of building

Once the King and Queen had settled on Kensington, they required the use of Nottingham House as soon as possible. Both the house and its service buildings, however, needed enlarging before they could be lived in: in spite of the abolition under Charles II of the ancient right of the whole household to dine at the King's expense – which allowed for a smaller building and establishment than would have been possible in earlier generations – the joint sovereigns required a far larger household than Lord Nottingham's. In addition, although it was their intention to live relatively simply at Kensington, they recognized that the house's winter use would make political gatherings unavoidable and therefore included a dedicated Council Chamber among the new rooms – something that the far grander palace at Hampton Court, used largely in summer, did not have.

Wren's response to the joint pressures of speed and economy was to retain at least the original part of Nottingham House and to add a rectangular block or 'pavilion' at each corner, just as Inigo Jones's prestigious successor, John Webb, had suggested for the enlargement of the Queen's House at Greenwich in the 1660s. The building accounts also refer to a "fifth pavilion", but where it stood is unknown.

Work began on site in early June 1689. The main building contracts – to Thomas Hughes, bricklayer, and John Hayward, carpenter, who were then expected to organize the labour force and sub-contract as necessary – were formalized on 3 July. With a view to economy, the main fabric was to be of brick – far cheaper than stone – with fashionable but expensive sash windows used only at first-floor level; clauses in the contracts ensured its speedy completion. Workshops and storage yards were set up nearby, and the site was taken over by an army of labourers and craftsmen, including bricklayers, carpenters, plasterers, tilers and plumbers, the latter responsible largely for roofing and the fitting of gutters and drains. Overall supervision was provided by Wren, operating from the Office of Works' headquarters in Scotland Yard, as much as he could be spared; day-to-day supervision was provided by Nicholas Hawksmoor and his deputies. A substantial amount of the paperwork produced in the process, such as estimates submitted by the Office of Works for approval by the King and his Treasury, accounts, tradesmen's bills, and plans and drawings, still survives and provides a vital source of information on the history of the house – as similar material does for other royal buildings (fig. 26). The work was paid for out of the annual income of £600,000 granted to William and Mary by Parliament in 1689. This money was drawn from the sovereign's historic revenues and from customs and post office receipts, all now in the control of Parliament; it was intended to cover not only the maintenance of the royal houses and household but also all the costs of government except defence. With the passing of the first Civil List Act in 1697, the relationship between the actual revenue and the amount granted to the King was regularized, his income being set in that year at a maximum of £700,000. Although the sums involved, their control and their intended purpose have altered, the essential logic of the system remains in place today.

Whilst the work was in progress in the autumn of 1689 the Queen herself was a regular visitor to Nottingham House, and, thanks partly to her constant urgings and a rapid expenditure of money, progress was very swift. But, as was also shown at Hampton Court in the same year, excessive speed had its penalties, and in November 1689 part of the new work collapsed. A journalist, with the sensationalism of his profession, reported that "the new apartment ... all of a sudden without warning given fell flat to the ground and has killed as I am tould 7 or 8 workmen or labourers", although, in reality, only one fatality occurred. A contemporary attributed the collapse to the presence of a vault beneath the new walls, but very probably – as is now known to have been the case at Hampton Court – it was due to an inadequate mortar mix, further weakened, perhaps, by cold weather. The Queen, apparently on site only hours before, was seriously shaken. Feeling partly responsible, she explained in a letter to the King that being unsettled at Holland House "made me go often to Kensington to hasten the Worckmen and I was too impatient to be [*i.e.* to live] at that place, imagining to find more ease there. This I often reproved myself for and at last it pleased God to shew me the uncertainty of all things ... for part of the house which was new built fell down."

Work on the house was not, however, seriously delayed, and by the end of November detailed arrangements were being made for its furnishing. This process was managed by the Great Wardrobe, the vast and complicated government department that since the Middle Ages had been responsible for storing and providing the king's goods. Under its supervision, new items were ordered from the leading furniture makers and suppliers of the day, and existing ones were brought over from Holland House and other royal houses and stores. Delivery was arranged by a sub-section of the department known as the Removing Wardrobe, which was also responsible for the cumbersome process of transporting the vast quantity of furnishings and equipment that accompanied the court when moving from house to house. Carriage was provided by the Board of Ordnance, which, charged with supplying and transporting the king's artillery, commanded a plentiful supply of horses and carts. Once the goods were on site, responsibility for distributing and caring for them was made over to the Housekeeper – in the case of Kensington, an old and much-favoured associate of William's called Simon de Brienne. On 24 December the King and Queen moved in – greatly to Mary's relief and satisfaction. She remarked in her memoirs, with very typical humility, "Blessed be the God who has at last after more than nine months being in England ... brought me to a place where I hope to be more at leisure to serve my maker."

The King's Apartments and their layout
The layout of the new residence, thanks to the inclusion of Nottingham House and its service annexes, had little of the symmetry that would have been expected even of a newly built country house. The main entrance to the house was not heralded by a formal, centrally placed approach, but by a modest timber *porte-cochère* of Tuscan columns (fig. 25) on the west side of the complex, completed in 1689 (since rebuilt). This opened into the 'Stone Gallery' – a corridor 55 m (180 ft) long enclosed within a

narrow block running eastwards to the south-west pavilion, with lodgings for important courtiers behind and above it. Facing this to the north was the Great Court (now usually called Clock Court), entered through an archway with a clock tower above (fig. 27), and enclosed to the north by a range of service buildings that included the new kitchens.

The far end of the Stone Gallery opened at the foot of the Great Stair, housed at this stage entirely within the south-west pavilion, and which led directly to the grandest rooms in the building. In these rooms the formal routines of court life and royal business were conducted (hence they were known to contemporaries as the State Apartments). The way in which the rooms were arranged at Kensington was based on a pattern that had been evolving, with various permutations and at different rates, in all the major royal residences of western Europe since the twelfth century. This was dictated by the function of State Apartments as a setting for the exercise and expression of the monarch's authority and the ceremonial and routines that grew up to support it; as these changed, therefore, so did the design of the apartments. A common purpose of their layout, however, was to control access to the sovereign, essentially so that he or she could remain ostensibly available to the many, while being provided with areas of restricted access for the conduct of state business and a degree of personal privacy. The main rooms were therefore usually arranged in a linear, interconnecting sequence, the extent of the visitor's advance into them (and of the sovereign's advance from the other direction) depending on rank; as the courtier

27. *View of the Great Court (or Clock Court), looking west. Designed by Wren, and also a product of the first phase of building, it was fully complete by April 1690; only the far part of the range to the right, built to replace Wren's kitchen in 1725, is later. Its unambitious scale and simple design is in keeping with the function and status of the house as the King intended in 1689.*

28. *Sir George Coppin's house at Kensington, viewed from the south-east, as it might have appeared when newly completed in about 1620 and much as William III would have first encountered it. The reconstruction is based on the surviving plan (fig. 9), the Sutton Nicholls engraving (fig. 23) and details borrowed from surviving buildings of the same period; it is guided by a reconstructed elevation prepared by Patrick Faulkner in 1948. The outbuildings and landscape details are entirely conjectural.*

29. *Reconstructed view of Kensington House as it might have looked from 1690 to 1695, taken from precisely the same vantage point as fig. 28. A four-floored 'pavilion' has been attached to each corner of the Jacobean house, which remained intact at the centre of the complex. To the left is the Stone Gallery range, much as it survives today, with the clock tower overlooking Clock Court appearing above it. The reconstruction demonstrates Wren's success not only in enlarging the house in a cheap and speedy manner, but also in creating a remarkably imposing effect.*

30. *View of Kensington House as it appeared after the King's Gallery range had been built across the south fronts of the two southern 'pavilions' in 1695. At this stage the Jacobean house still survived, although by then only clearly visible from the north; it was later destroyed and replaced by the structure that still exists at the centre of the State Apartments, which extended eastwards to fill the gap between the two right-hand 'pavilions', creating the east-facing elevation that survives today (fig. 70).*

32. *Portrait of Hans Willem Bentinck, 1st Earl of Portland, from the studio of Hyacinthe Rigaud, 1698–99. The Earl of Portland was William III's chief favourite until the late 1690s and held the important offices of Groom of the Stole, Keeper of the Privy Purse and Superintendent of the Royal Gardens. He was allocated very substantial apartments in the royal residences, including Kensington Palace.*

Official business also extended to receiving foreign dignitaries and ambassadors, occasions on which the full ceremonial machinery of the State Apartments was brought into play. Such visitors were often also entertained to dinner, a meal that began in the mid-afternoon but could last for many hours; it was held in the private apartments, with any necessary furniture brought in for the occasion. Visitors of royal rank might dine with the King 'in public' – in other words, on their own, with great formality, in one of the 'public' or outer rooms of the State Apartments – although William avoided this at Kensington. Records kept by the Lord Steward's Department give a minutely detailed picture of the vast range and quantity of food and drink brought to Kensington on a regular basis and consumed by the sovereigns and their household. Once or twice a week an opportunity was given for the sovereigns' subjects to see and perhaps talk to them; this took the form of an audience, normally held in the Presence Chamber. Opportunities for courtiers and high-ranking members of society to meet the King and Queen were also offered by the regular gatherings held in the Queen's Drawing Room. These were particularly valued, at Kensington as elsewhere, for the relative informality permitted in the Queen's Apartments, an attribute that does much to explain why it was Mary, rather than William, who was provided with a Drawing Room within the limited space of their new house. In later reigns the 'Drawing Room', named after the room in which it took place, was to become the main public event of court life (see below). There were also plenty of events intended for entertainment, usually in honour of an occasion such as the King's birthday or the arrival of an important guest; the most spectacular of these were balls, of which fourteen were held at Kensington between 1691 and 1694. A description of one in January 1694 gives a flavour of what they were like:

> Saturday night last was a great entertainment made for the Prince of Baden at Kensington, where was dancing and gaming, and a great supper; and banquets of sweetmeats all common to such as were admitted to be spectators. And I was informed by one that was present, that hee supposed there could not be less than 1000 persons, but it was 5 of the clock in the morning before some of them could get home.

Social activity as a whole at Kensington appears to have diminished after Mary's death in 1694, but in the late 1690s a new emphasis seems to have been laid on musical and theatrical entertainments. In 1698 a stage was fitted up for "a performance of Musick before his Majesty at Kensington", and furniture was ordered for "the new theatre at Kensington", probably contrived within the old Nottingham House. In November 1698 the Lord Chamberlain ordered the completion of a "stage for performing operas". What pieces were played and performed, or by whom, is not recorded, but possibly the work of Henry Purcell, who had written *Dido and Aeneas* in the year of the King's accession, was fairly represented. The Master of the Music, Nicholas Staggins, and his musicians – members of the Lord Chamberlain's Department – must also have made a contribution.

Courtiers' accommodation and service areas

William's great favourite, Hans Willem Bentinck, 1st Earl of Portland, Groom of the Stole and holder of a wide range of other offices, was lodged close to the King on the ground floor of the old Nottingham House, as was the Master of the Horse, Henry of Nassau, but most of the accommodation required by the main household at Kensington had to be provided from scratch. The Lord Chamberlain and the Lord Steward were lodged in the Stone Gallery range, along with a variety of lesser officials. Other officials' residences were scattered about elsewhere, such as on the ground floor of the Queen's Gallery range and in the corner pavilions.

The remainder of the domestic buildings as they existed under William and Mary were taken up by the offices, stores and kitchens needed to supply the household with food and other necessities such as linen, fuel and lighting. Some of these had been inherited with Nottingham House, including the two north–south ranges, of mixed purpose but including the Earl's kitchens, which enclosed what was then called the Kitchen Court (rebuilt in 1725 and renamed the Prince of Wales's Court). The kitchen

itself, however, was built from new and formed the west part of the north side of the new Clock Court (fig. 50). Within the immediate orbit of the palace, accommodation had also to be provided for the military detachments responsible for the sovereign's safety. In William's time these consisted of three troops of Horse Guards and one of mounted Grenadiers, each troop (about twenty men) taking a week's duty in turn, and one of Foot Guards. From 1689/90 until at least 1714 the Horse Guards were housed in the two-storey building put up to the south-west of the house, facing Palace Green, which still survives (fig. 35). In 1696 a second building was erected for their use, standing on a north–south axis immediately to the north of the palace, which contained stabling at ground level with the men's quarters above (fig. 34). The Foot Guards meanwhile were put up in the two-storey north–south building due west of the main entrance to the house (fig. 33).

No great house, let alone a royal one, could exist without its stables and coach houses, and Kensington was swiftly provided with both. For a short while Lord Nottingham's stables and coach house were retained, but these were completely replaced in 1690; ten years later the new ones were enlarged, as a result of which the complex enclosed or partially enclosed three vast courtyards immediately to the north of the palace (fig. 34). The management of the stables was in the hands of Simon de Brienne, in his second capacity as Surveyor of His Majesty's Stables at Kensington, with the exception of the military block, supervised by the Master of the Horse. Working for them, and in some cases lodged in the stable courtyards, were many of the vast numbers of grooms, farriers, coachmen and others who looked after the horses and vehicles.

The Queen's Apartments

Mary's apartments lay in the north-west pavilion, although they extended into the old Nottingham House, which contained the Presence Chamber that she shared with the King. Beyond that lay the Withdrawing Room and its anteroom, a Bedchamber, a closet, an "inward closett", and a Dressing Room and its anteroom. As shown by the furnishing list of December 1689, the rooms were equipped with a mixture of new items and others removed from

TOP LEFT 33. *The Foot Guards' barracks, built to the west of the palace in the 1690s. At the time this amateur drawing was made, in the second half of the eighteenth century, the building was in use as the Guards' canteen (see fig. 58).*

ABOVE LEFT 34. *Plan of the stable yards, coach houses and related buildings standing immediately to the north of the house as they existed in the early years of George I's reign. The north–south building containing a row of stalls was the second Horse Guards' barrack block, built in 1696; the square building to the south was a kitchen block built in 1698–99 for Arnold Joost van Keppel, by then 1st Earl of Albemarle, Groom of the Bedchamber, Master of the Robes and one of William's closest companions.*

ABOVE RIGHT 35. *The barrack block at the south end of Palace Green, built for the Horse Guards who formed the major part of the King's Guard at Kensington in 1689–90. It contained stabling on the ground floor with the men's accommodation above.*

33

LEFT 36. *View from the north-east of the wing added to enlarge the Queen's Apartments at Kensington in 1690. The doorway opens at the foot of the Queen's Staircase, providing independent access between the apartments and the gardens.*

BELOW LEFT 37. *The Queen's Eating Room, used by William and Mary for informal dining. It lies within the original north-west pavilion, adjacent to the back stairs that linked it to the kitchens, but took on the function of a dining room only after the extension of the Queen's Apartments in 1692. In Mary's time it was furnished with walnut chairs and stools, screens to ward off draughts, and with crimson damask curtains. Since then the room has been reduced in size and the panelling altered, although the fireplace remains unchanged.*

BELOW RIGHT 38. *One of the two fireplaces and overmantels in the Queen's Gallery. Although somewhat altered (compare with fig. 2), the overmantel, made by Grinling Gibbons, is a rare survival of the giltwood furniture used by Mary II to display porcelain. The mirrored glass was supplied by the cabinet-maker Gerrit Jensen, and the marble fire-surround below by the mason Thomas Hill.*

OPPOSITE 39. *The Queen's Staircase, little changed since its construction in 1690–91.*

40. *Engraving of a 'china-closet', published by the great designer Daniel Marot in 1702. Mary II had rooms very like this at Het Loo, and the smaller rooms in the Queen's Apartments at Kensington probably looked very similar in the early 1690s.*

St James's Palace, Whitehall and Hampton Court and brought over from Holland House.

In the summer of 1690, however, with the new apartments barely complete, the Queen set about extending them. It was perhaps a curious moment to choose. In March 1690, in a bid to regain the English throne, James II had landed in Ireland with French help and French troops, and in June King William had embarked on the campaign that culminated in victory on the Boyne river – a bright moment in a year of Anglo-Dutch defeats elsewhere. Given Mary's duties as Head of State in the King's absence and her truly desperate worries for his safety, the new building campaign was perhaps a welcome diversion. In any case, work began in June 1690 with alterations to the existing rooms, to which the new building was to be attached, and was finished in March 1691. The 'new' building, a long narrow range of two floors over a basement, with a short westward extension at the north end (fig. 36), was not entirely new: recent archaeological investigation in the roof space above the Queen's Gallery has shown that it incorporated an earlier block – perhaps Wren's 'fifth pavilion', or a block added to the original house by the Finches. As usual the most important rooms were upstairs, accessible from the existing house but also provided

with independent external access to the north by means of a staircase and doorway (figs. 36, 39). The largest room was the gallery, which took up the whole width of the range and was 25.6 m (84 ft) long. By Mary's time, a gallery was used essentially for the display of works of art, but the concept of such a room originated in the raised passages linking parts of medieval buildings, and more immediately in the Tudor and Jacobean 'long gallery'.

The progress of the new building work was followed closely by the Queen, who came out regularly from Whitehall to view it, as well as "for the air". In spite of the worries expressed in letters to the King that this work and some minor improvements to his own apartments would not be finished on time, they were ready for his triumphant return to Kensington on 10 September.

Queen Mary's Far Eastern collection

The interiors of the new and refurbished rooms – fitted out by the carpenter Alexander Fort, the mason and sculptor Thomas Hill and the carvers Nicholas Alcock, William Emmett and Grinling Gibbons – were of good quality but not extravagant, with careful use being made of features salvaged from the 'old' apartments. Queen Mary's decorative and furnishing

ABOVE 41. *A pair of hexagonal 'Hampton Court jars', named after the examples kept there since c. 1700 and made by the Japanese Kakiemon factory in the late seventeenth century. The "coloured Jarrs of 6 squares" mentioned in the Kensington inventory of 1693 were probably of this type.*

RIGHT 42. *One of a set of panels embroidered in wool to a design by Daniel Marot and originally used at Hampton Court, where they are now on display. These represent the type of professionally made work that Mary hung on the walls of the gallery at Kensington, bordered with red, black and white velvet.*

scheme, to which the new work provided a backdrop, was perhaps the most remarkable ever achieved at Kensington. The key ingredient was porcelain. Known in Europe since the sixteenth century, in the early seventeenth century it was used as tableware, thanks to the deliberate Chinese production of European shapes. In the middle of the century, however, civil war in China ended the production of export wares, leaving available only material intended for the home market. Oriental eating habits being rather different, this was of no use in Europe, but the resulting products remained highly prized for their decorative value – hence the origin of the 'Porcelain Room', decorated almost exclusively with porcelain or intended for its display. When, after 1658, the Dutch turned to Japanese suppliers, decorative and useable items were equally in demand.

Mary's knowledge of and enthusiasm for porcelain and Oriental applied art in general had been fostered in Holland, then dominating control of Far Eastern trade, and she had made lavish use of it in her Dutch houses such as Honselaarsdijk and Het Loo (fig. 40). Given the opportunities and resources offered to her after 1689, it was natural that she should do so in England. Some of what she displayed here – either brought over from Holland,

These Engins, (which are ... the best) to quench great Fires; are

JOHN KEELING

43. *Engraving of 1678 showing a pump or 'engine', probably similar to those brought over from Whitehall to fight the fire at Kensington in 1692. Given the time it took for them to arrive and their limitations, the house had a very narrow escape.*

purchased new or inherited – was displayed in the Tudor 'Water Gallery' by the Thames at Hampton Court, lavishly refitted in 1689–90. The bulk of the collection, however, was reserved for Kensington, where it occupied not just one but five of Mary's new rooms. The most richly supplied was the gallery, which contained 154 pieces of porcelain: nineteen over each fireplace, nine over two doors and seven over the other two, the remainder arranged on shelves and pedestals and massed in great symmetrical arrangements on the tops of lacquer cabinets. The result was a supreme example of what Daniel Defoe – although not an admirer – described as "the Custom or Humour, as I may call it, of furnishing houses with China-Ware, which increased to a strange degree afterwards, piling their China on the Tops of Cabinets, Scrutores [writing-desks], and every Chymney-Piece, to the tops of the Ceilings, and even setting up shelves for their China-Ware".

Of the other furnishings, much was also Oriental or in an Oriental style, and included printed cottons from India and lacquered furniture (either made and lacquered in Japan, made up in Europe from genuine panels or 'japanned' in imitation). The walls of the gallery were covered with crimson velvet hangings, embellished with appliqué velvet pillars and embroidered festoons, and with the splendid mirrors by Gerrit Jensen that can still be seen there today (fig. 38). The overall effect, not least by candlelight, must have been extraordinarily rich and exotic.

The fire of 1692

The last major building works to the main house before Queen Mary's death were repairs after a fire that nearly destroyed it, as was to be the fate of Whitehall Palace six years later. The fire broke out in the Stone Gallery range on 11 November 1692, apparently "thro' the carelessness of a candle", and quickly spread. The King and Queen, both there at the time, were seriously alarmed – the King, fearing first a plot and then the loss of his new house and its contents, ordered the evacuation of his best pictures and the Queen's porcelain. In the event, although the Earl of Portland's lodgings and those of other important courtiers were completely wrecked, the main house was saved. But it was a lucky escape, as there were no 'water-engines' or other fire-fighting equipment (quite sophisticated by this date: fig. 43) at Kensington; these had, therefore, to be summoned from Whitehall. The fire meanwhile had been tackled by soldiers from the barracks with water carried in broken-open bottles from the beer-cellar. Once again Mary was humbled by the experience, confessing in her memoirs that "I had to much in the convenience of my house and neatness of my furniture, and I was taught a second time the vanity of all such things." The repair work and the massive job of clearing tons of debris continued until July of the following year.

Meanwhile, in April 1692, a more imposing introduction to the royal apartments from the Great Court was provided by a two-storey stone block that spanned the gap between the two western pavilions.

This provided a link between the pavilions at first- and ground-floor levels, allowing easier access, via the Great Stair, to the Queen's Apartments; these too were enlarged by the heightening of the adjoining northern Great Court range at its east end, which today remains a storey higher than the rest. The Great Stair for the moment remained as built in 1689, but the Guard Chamber, formerly upstairs within the south-west pavilion, was relocated downstairs at the east end of the Stone Gallery range. It would appear to have risen through the height of two storeys and been overlooked by a gallery or balcony.

The gardens at Kensington

The improvement and enlargement of the gardens at Kensington was, from a practical point of view, much less urgent than that of the house, not least as the Finches' gardens were already very fine. They must have suffered, however, during the first phase of building works and again with the addition of the King's Gallery range in 1695, while the intrusion of the new buildings and increased traffic made some changes necessary in any case. Not surprisingly, the earliest accounts are for ground works and the making and gravelling of paths. Major improvements to the design and planting of the garden, however, soon followed. According to Defoe, who claimed to have inspected the site in the Queen's company, "The first laying out of these Gardens was the design of the late Queen Mary, who finding the Air agreed with, and was necessary to the Health of the King, resolved to make it agreeable to her self too, and gave the first Orders for enlarging the Gardens."

Whether the area of actual garden (as opposed to grassland and orchard) was really much increased is not clear, but Mary's role in initiating the improvement was all-important. Both she and William had taken a great interest in gardens in Holland, for example improving those at Honselaarsdijk and creating those at Het Loo (fig. 45) from scratch; they were also expert plantsmen and very conscious of the latest fashions in garden design. For practical purposes, however, control of the work at Kensington was in the hands of the Earl of Portland, already Superintendent of the Stadtholder's gardens and, since April 1689, Superintendent of the Royal Gardens. As his deputy he had swiftly chosen George London, England's leading garden designer and since 1689 joint owner with Henry Wise of a great commercial nursery at Brompton Park. London and Wise's joint domination of royal garden design, their role in its execution and their presence at Kensington were to last well into the eighteenth century.

What they actually did there, however, is more problematic since, in the absence of contemporary plans, views or detailed descriptions, we have to rely on the accounts – very precise when it comes to how much was spent, but less so on where the money went. A process of elimination, however, places the greatest area of activity between 1690 and 1696 to the south of the house, for an agreement of 1690 made over the use of the land to the north to the Housekeeper, de Brienne, while that to the west and south-west remained in use as service yards and kitchen gardens. Whether the whole of the southern area was taken up by garden is unclear, but there are hints in the accounts that features towards the southern end of Queen Anne's garden (fig. 58) dated from William's time and thus had been achieved at the latest by 1702. In any case, the new work included heavy expenditure on gravel walks and flanking

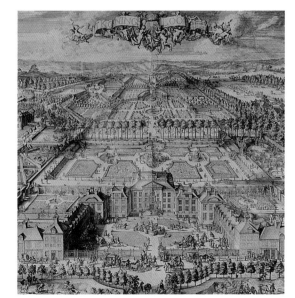

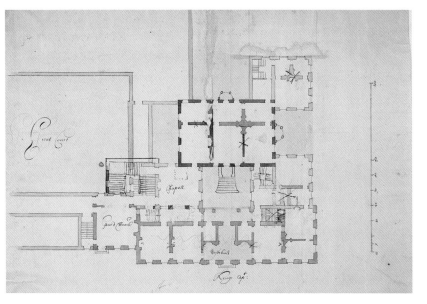

TOP 46. *Large print or 'broadsheet' produced by Romeyn de Hooghe in or shortly after December 1694, representing the last hours of Mary II. The details of the room and its furniture are probably fanciful (although Mary's must have been similar), but the size of the attendant throng and its composition is accurate enough; it includes, to the extreme left, the Queen's doctors and, sitting opposite them, the Archbishop of Canterbury. The King himself can be seen coming into the room followed by a group of Privy Councillors.*

MIDDLE 47. *Plan dating from the first months of 1695, showing (in red) the position and ground-floor layout of the range housing the King's Gallery as actually executed. The position of the King's Stair as rebuilt in the following year has been sketched in, either in anticipation of its reconstruction or at a later date.*

BOTTOM 48. *The South Front or King's Gallery range added to Kensington House in 1695.*

borders and reflects the sovereigns' Dutch tastes in the vast number and variety of trees and plants. Other areas of garden were certainly also improved – probably including those overlooked by the Queen's Gallery, perhaps the 'new flower garden', "the Queen's little garden" mentioned in the accounts.

Further expansion of the garden area seems to have come only in 1701. In that year George London was ordered to set about "trenching, new-making and planting that part of Kensington gardens that formerly was an old orchard", conceivably to the south of the house – and thus the extension that first took it down to the Hammersmith Road – but more probably to the north-west. The borders were planted with pyramid-shaped evergreens, and the 'quarters' – defined by paths and hedges – with a wide variety of shrubs.

For all this, the extent and grandeur of Kensington Gardens before 1702 remained in keeping with the modest semi-private use of the house; it would be in the next reign and later that they would take their place among the greatest royal gardens in the country.

The King alone, 1694–1702

The death of Queen Mary

Waking up at Kensington on the morning of 21 December 1694 Mary felt unwell, noticed a rash on her arms and correctly recognized the symptoms of smallpox – then prevalent in London, and usually fatal. With great calm she put her papers in order, wrote instructions for her funeral and inventoried her jewels. Within a few days it was clear that in spite of – or perhaps as a result of – her doctors' treatments (they included bleeding and burning with hot irons) recovery was impossible. Although they had married for dynastic reasons, as time passed William and

Mary became deeply attached to each other, as their correspondence shows. In contrast to Mary's calm, the King was greatly distressed, the normally dour and reserved man astonishing his hearers on receiving the news that "from being the happiest, he was now going to be the miserablest creature on earth". He said, according to the contemporary author Gilbert Burnet, that "during the whole course of their marriage, he had never known one single fault in her", and spent the last few days of the Queen's life on a camp bed in her room. When she died on the 28th, many assumed

that the distraught King would swiftly follow her.

An important architectural consequence of the Queen's death was William's abandonment, hastened by a chronic shortage of funds, of building work at Hampton Court. Without Mary's encouragement the great rooms were left empty and unfinished, until the burning down of Whitehall in 1698 made the resumption of work necessary. Meanwhile, William's efforts were concentrated on Kensington, where he embarked on the building programme that gave the house its existing South Front.

The King's Gallery and the King's Stair

In the spring of 1695 William embarked upon the last major addition to the palace before the 1720s: a range extending across the south of the house, concealing the two southern pavilions and enclosing the space between them – now known as White Court. The new work was prompted by the King's increased use of Kensington, the desire to improve his quarters and to give the house an architectural dignity it so far lacked. In addition, it reflected William's artistic interests, for the main room of the new wing, extending the full length of its top floor, was to be his gallery. The original intention or suggestion seems to have been for a very ambitious project indeed, for in 1814 the antiquary John Nichols not only reported the existence of a drawing for an elevation of three storeys and an attic, with "a centre, continuation right and left wings", but also inferred that the East Front was to be rebuilt. Nevertheless, no doubt influenced by the usual constraint of time and certainly by lack of money, it was a contract for a more modest structure that was signed with the bricklayer, Richard Stacey, on 29 April and the work was finished in the autumn of the following year. The design was undoubtedly by Wren, although Hawksmoor, as Clerk of Works, may have had a creative hand in it; certainly he was paid £5 2s for "pastboard and other materials for making a Modell of the said Gallery", presumably submitted to the King for his approval. The resulting elevation, eleven windows across and entirely of brick, was very plain, enriched only at the centre with four brick pilasters, carried upwards as an 'attic' and crowned with "iiii great fflower pots of Portland stone richly carved". The design of the centrepiece, derived ultimately from the Roman triumphal arch, was similar, although with vital differences, to the central enrichment to the South Front at Hampton Court. Today the façade remains unchanged, except that the original sashes, replaced in the nineteenth century, were not painted but of varnished oak, and the cornice (now an off-white) was painted to look like stone, perhaps with touches of colour. Plain as it is, however, it was and remains the palace's only formal, 'set-piece' façade.

The interior decoration of the King's Gallery as it is today, although perhaps the most splendid in the palace, dates from the 1720s (fig. 81), and all that now remains from Wren's time are the carved cornice, the dado panelling and the remarkable wind-dial or 'anemoscope' over the fireplace (fig. 49). The seventy-one pictures William hung there, however, are known from a list made in 1697 and included some of the very best in the royal collection: among them, at least according to the attributions of the time, were seven paintings by the great Venetian master Titian, a Leonardo, two Michelangelos and the famous portrait of Charles I and his family by Sir Anthony van Dyck,

now at Buckingham Palace. William himself, as was his habit, took a keen interest in the selection and hanging of the pictures, asking his friend Constantijn Huygens that they should be hung on ropes to allow for easy rearrangement.

Following the completion of the gallery, the 'Great' or King's Stair was replaced by the existing structure, built on a larger scale in stone and accommodated by extending the south-west pavilion out into Clock Court. Although the painted decoration is later, all but a small part of the wrought-iron balustrade, for which the celebrated ironworker Jean Tijou was paid in September 1696, is original.

Apartments for a new queen?

As William and Mary had had no children, the heir to the throne at Mary's death in 1694 was her sister, Anne. She, in turn, would have been succeeded by her son, William Henry, Duke of Gloucester, to whom, in the spring of 1700, William granted Mary's former apartments at Kensington. When the boy died in July of the same year (a process aided, as was usual with royal deaths in the seventeenth and eighteenth centuries, by his doctors) William was deeply upset. But he was also faced with renewed uncertainties as to who would succeed Anne, not now expected to have any further children, a problem worsened by the existence of contenders from abroad – particularly James II's son, James Francis Edward Stuart. The issue was eventually to be resolved by the Act of Settlement of 1701, by which the Electress Sophia of Hanover and her descendants were named as Anne's successors. In the years immediately following Mary's death, however, the King came quite close to marrying again, with the aim of providing a Protestant heir to Anne. In 1696 the Earl of Portland arranged for the King to meet the fourteen-year-old daughter of Frederick, Elector of Brandenburg, and the King was reported to be buying new furniture for Kensington, causing people to assume that a marriage was imminent. In the end the project came to nothing, but it is the best explanation for a scheme to attach an entirely new wing to the palace, extending southwards from the west end of the new King's Gallery range, that would contain a complete suite of State Apartments from Guard Chamber to closet (fig. 51). These were laid out in a more ambitious and advanced fashion than the King's Apartments as they then existed and included, clearly labelled and between the Privy Chamber and Bedchamber, a 'Drawing Room'.

The last days of King William

Kensington House, on which William had lavished so much attention throughout his reign and to which he had grown so attached, was also the scene of the King's last moments, on 8 March 1702. The story

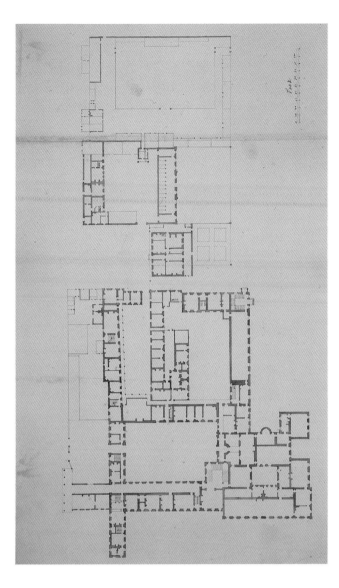

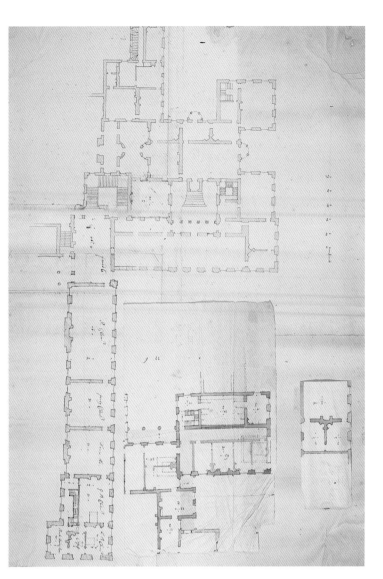

ABOVE LEFT 50. *Plan of the entire palace complex almost exactly as left by William III, drawn between 1706 and 1718. Roughly speaking, the State Apartments are shown at top-floor level (that of the main rooms), but other areas, including the Stone Gallery range and the stables to the north, are at ground-floor level.*

ABOVE RIGHT 51. *Contemporary plan for a new wing, extending southwards at right angles to the King's Gallery range, prepared in the summer of 1696, at a time when William was expected to take a second wife, and possibly intended for her use. The detail shown at lower right relates to a separate scheme.*

that he died as a result of a fall while riding in Hampton Court or Bushy Park, when his horse stumbled on a molehill, is well known. Whether, in fact, there was a link between this and his death nearly three weeks later is not really clear. Certainly the real details of the accident differ slightly from the popular version; his own account suggests that his horse's off-front foot broke through the surface – perhaps into a mole-run – and that "falling first forward and then sideways", the King landed on his right shoulder and broke his collarbone. That evening William went by carriage to Kensington where, although the fracture had to be reset on arrival, he made a slow recovery over the next few days, sustained by an alcoholic 'cordial' supposedly invented by Sir Walter Ralegh when imprisoned in the Tower of London. In the first days of March, however, he was struck down by a fever and respiratory problems and on the 6th, after taking some exercise in the King's Gallery, fell asleep on a chair near an open window and caught a chill. He died two days later, his

chamber packed with courtiers and his favourite, the Earl of Albemarle – unlike Portland, who was too late – arriving just in time to hear his last confidences. The King's body was removed to Westminster for the lying in state, and Kensington was decked out in mourning, with black and purple cloth covering the floors, walls and furniture. Within a month, though, all this was removed, as court officials were awarded their traditional perks: the crimson damask and gold lace bed in the 'new little Bedchamber' in which the King had died, for example, together with the entire contents of the room, were given by the new Queen to William's Groom of the Stole, the Earl of Romney.

KENSINGTON *under*
QUEEN ANNE 1702–14

Kensington becomes a favoured home of Queen Anne; as sovereign she occupies the King's Apartments, and the Queen's Apartments are adapted for her consort, Prince George of Denmark. Vast new gardens are laid out, and the magnificent Orangery is built to the designs of Nicholas Hawksmoor. The Queen's celebrated friendship with the Duchess of Marlborough comes to a stormy end at Kensington in 1710.

52. Sir Godfrey Kneller's portrait of Queen Anne with her son, William, Duke of Gloucester, painted in about 1694. The little duke was much liked by his uncle, William III, who astonished his courtiers by joining in the child's games. His death in 1700 led to the eventual succession of George I.

Queen Anne and her reign

One of King William's last acts was to approve the formal barring of the claim of the 'Old Pretender', James Francis Edward Stuart, to be William's successor, and although the King refused Princess Anne's request to visit him at Kensington, her accession was not in doubt. The news of the King's death was brought to her at St James's Palace by Gilbert Burnet, Bishop of Salisbury – a breach of protocol, which, carried out in the hopes of pleasing her, earned him the ridicule of the court and the Queen's fury. She spent the remainder of the morning at St James's, besieged by a vast throng of people trying to make themselves known to her and receiving a few of them at a select *levée*, while the Privy Council assembled. In scenes foreshadowing those of 1837, the new Queen impressed both the Privy Council and the joint Houses of Parliament with her presence and the delivery of her speeches (thanks partly to voice training, arranged years before by Charles II). During the remainder of her reign, although she never sustained a real command of state affairs, Anne's fervent patriotism, prominent support for the Anglican Church and her studied Englishness all helped her to become a respected and effective sovereign.

In politics, Anne tried, like William, to steer a middle path between the Whig and Tory factions, and until 1710 successfully governed through a coalition, although it was increasingly Whig in composition. Her support for politicians, however, was heavily influenced by personal preferences, and she continued to favour, for example, the Tory leader and political survivor *par excellence* Robert Harley, Earl of Oxford, even when he was in disgrace. For a similar reason the main political influence on the Queen, as in other matters, was Sarah Churchill. Her personal hold on Anne, and the successive victories and apparent indispensability of her husband, the Duke of Marlborough, steadily increased Anne's support for the Whigs.

On the international stage, the War of the Spanish Succession was concluded in 1713, thanks very largely to Marlborough's great victories at Blenheim (1704), Ramillies (1706) and Malplaquet (1709); victory was

sealed with the Treaty of Utrecht, by which England confirmed its claim to Gibraltar, received territories in the Americas and, less gloriously but to the great profit of Bristol and Liverpool, gained control of the Atlantic slave trade. Closer to home, the Act of Union of 1707 saw England and Scotland formally united under a single parliament.

In Anne's personal life, the Duchess of Marlborough was also her greatest and her only real friend. The two had met as children at the court of Charles II, and the highly articulate and forceful Sarah soon captivated the timid young princess. When Anne succeeded, they agreed to refer to each other as 'Mrs Morley' and 'Mrs Freeman' to keep themselves from being distanced by her new status. Their vast correspondence shows how dependent Anne was on the Duchess, the Queen letting her know on more than one occasion that "I can not live without you." The Duchess, however, increasingly abused her position, both personally and in the advancement of her family. As Keeper of the Privy Purse she also managed to keep the Queen helplessly short of money, and in later years treated the sick, childless woman with open contempt. With the backing of the political opposition, in 1707 a junior lady-in-waiting, Abigail Hill (later Lady Masham), began to usurp the Duchess in the Queen's favour and attention and in 1708 moved into Sarah's rooms at Kensington. Provoked by this and other signs of falling out of favour the Duchess complained bitterly, but it was too late, the Queen responding that "she desired nothing but that she would leave off teasing and tormenting" her. The end came in a tearful scene in April 1710 when the Duchess pursued the Queen to Kensington, confronted her in one of her closets, demanded to know what she was accused of and was rebuffed in a few words. They never met again. In the following year, in the midst of a range of political complications, the Duchess and her husband were formally dismissed from all offices (fig. 53).

From 1683 until his death in 1708, Anne enjoyed a happy marriage to Prince George, second son of Frederick III of Denmark. Their family life, however,

RIGHT 53. *A playing card of 1711, or shortly after, showing Queen Anne (seated) in the act of bestowing the Office of Groom of the Stole on Elizabeth Seymour, Duchess of Somerset, wife of Anne's Master of the Horse. This office, among others, had previously been held by the Duchess of Marlborough, with whom the Queen had finally fallen out in the previous year. Intrigue at court, closely intertwined as it was with politics, was closely followed in the popular press and publicized in other printed material.*

BELOW 54. *George of Denmark depicted in the role of Lord High Admiral by Antonio Verrio in the Queen's Apartments at Hampton Court which, as consort, he had the use of. The martial image was hardly realistic, as the lethargic Prince, in the words of a contemporary journalist, loved "only news, the bottle and the Queen".*

*Vpon her Knees fam'd Somerset receives,
An Office which another D____fs leaves.*

was tragic. Between 1684 and 1695 Anne had twelve miscarriages and two children who lived only a few hours. In 1689 she had a son, William, Duke of Gloucester, who was stronger than his siblings but nonetheless lived only until 1700. The young Prince's death immediately raised, once again, the need to secure a Protestant succession. The best claim would have lain with James II's twelve-year-old son, James Francis Edward Stuart, but he refused to give up his Catholicism. Among the many potential Protestant successors, King William's preference had been for Sophia, Dowager Electress of Hanover, partly because her north German state would have made a useful ally for the Dutch against the French. As Elector, her husband had been one of the small group of rulers who nominally controlled the selection of the Holy Roman Emperor. Sophia's claim came through her mother, James I's daughter Elizabeth, the unfortunate 'Winter Queen' of Bohemia who had married Frederick, the Elector of the Rhineland Palatinate, in 1613, and in 1619 was exiled with him after his short reign as King of Bohemia. Visiting Sophia in 1700, however, William found her less than keen – not least because she openly supported the claim of James Francis Edward Stuart – but within a year, encouraged by her son, she had grown more enthusiastic; in June 1701, the Act of Settlement formally named her and her successors as heirs to the English throne.

Queen Anne herself, not surprisingly, was usually unwell. In the last years of her reign her health rapidly deteriorated and she was unable to walk unaided, although she continued to follow the hunt in a fast carriage. In July 1714, already exhausted by political difficulties centred on a resurgence of Jacobite support, she became fatally ill. Although the Hanoverian succession had in theory long been settled, it was only through political manoeuvring at the Queen's bedside at Kensington that it was finally assured with the appointment of the prominent Whig Charles Talbot, Earl of Shrewsbury, as Lord Treasurer. Her end hastened, according to one of her official doctors, John Arbuthnot, by "the last troublesome scene of contention among her servants", the Queen died on 1 August. In a letter to Jonathan Swift, Arbuthnot wrote that he believed "sleep was never more welcome to a weary traveller than death was to her". As Sophia of Hanover had died two months before, her son, George Lewis, was now King, and the Regency Council, which he had had a hand in selecting, came into force.

The Queen and Kensington
The Queen's use of Kensington
Queen Anne knew Kensington House and its surroundings very well, having had the use of nearby Campden House since 1689, in addition to lodgings at Whitehall and, after 1694, at St James's Palace. Unlike William, however, she had no particular aversion to

55. *Aerial view of the entrance front of Blenheim Palace, built for John Churchill, Duke of Marlborough, in gratitude for his great victory in 1704 and as a national monument. The single greatest house of the period, Blenheim was designed by Vanbrugh and Hawksmoor, both of whom also worked on schemes for Kensington.*

56. *Aerial view of Kensington Palace from the south-west, taken in 2002. Although the surroundings of the palace have changed considerably since the time of George I, the general form of the building remains much as he left it: in the foreground are the King's Gallery of 1695 and, to the left, the Stone Gallery range, a remnant of Wren's work of 1689–90; behind it is Clock Court, and beyond that are the Prince of Wales's and the Princesses' Courts, both largely of the 1720s. Further to the north lie the former stables and coach houses and, to the far right, the Orangery of 1704–05.*

staying at St James's during the busy winter period, nor did she abandon London for the country as soon as it was over; when she did, in a similar reversal of William's practice, she preferred Windsor to Hampton Court. In the first years of her reign her creative intentions focused on Whitehall, which, like William, she seriously considered rebuilding: according to Luttrell's entry in his *Brief Historical Relation* for 6 October 1702, it was being said that she intended to complete it in six years, making Kensington over to Prince George as a purely private residence.

Initially, the Queen used Kensington for recreation more than for business and until 1705 only made day visits, although she dined there often enough to require a permanent kitchen staff. Occasionally she stayed a few days, in which case part of the court and the vast supporting cast of courtiers and servants went with her. From 1705 she spent longer periods there, including one of nine months from September 1706, perhaps encouraged by the improvements she had made to the gardens and certainly by the benefits of Kensington's clean air to Prince George who was, like William III, an asthmatic. From September 1707 until June 1708 they were almost continually at Kensington and returned there again from Windsor in September. This was, however, to be their last stay together as Prince George died at the palace on 28 October and, dissuaded by the Duchess of Marlborough from remaining there, the Queen left that day for St James's. For eighteen months she stayed away but returned for the spring and early summer of the last four years of her reign.

Building works and decoration
Changing and increasing use of the house required a virtually continuous series of minor improvements throughout the reign. Overall responsibility for most of these still lay with Wren and Hawksmoor; the latter, Clerk of Works for Kensington since 1689 and assisted by a 'Labourer in Trust' or foreman, was in control of work on site. The only major change to the hierarchy of the Office of Works took place in 1702, when Talman was replaced as Comptroller by John Vanbrugh, a relative newcomer to the profession but one whose bold and theatrical architecture was in keeping with his previous careers as a soldier and playwright. Wren, Hawksmoor and Vanbrugh were provided with houses at the edge of the grounds to the south-west, although only Hawksmoor made use of his.

At the beginning of Anne's reign, in order to make the house usable at all, the last phase of redecoration and rearrangement that William III had ordered for his own apartments had to be completed: as sovereign, Anne used and occupied the King's Apartments (at least for formal business) as Elizabeth I and Mary I had done at their palaces. At that time, as Wren reported to the Treasury in the summer of 1706, the

Queen had also considered some fairly major additions and alterations, including the addition of "severall New Rooms ... in the Little Court behind the Gallery ... together with a new Drawing room". In the end the "New Rooms" were the only part to be completed, but a plan that shows them as built, and also an unexecuted expansion of the King's Apartments, feasibly including a Drawing Room (fig. 50), may have been prepared as a result. The Queen's intention to include a Drawing Room, however, shows her awareness that the main apartments lacked what was by then the principal setting for most regular 'public' occasions at court – an omission finally put right in the next reign.

In addition to improving the Queen's lodgings, a great deal of work, although more decorative than structural, was carried out over the next few years to fit up apartments for Prince George. These were largely, as befitted the consort, those of the former Queen, which in 1700 had been granted to the little Duke of Gloucester but had laid largely empty since his death. As a result, the Queen's Gallery range was usually known, from then until well into the twentieth century, as the 'Denmark Wing'. It seems that Prince George was also given part of "the lodgings that were my Lord Albemarle's", as these are referred to in the accounts for 1702–03 as now being "the Prince's". As Albemarle's apartments offered rather easier communication with the King's rooms than Queen Mary's did, this allowed the Prince and the Queen a private life that, for royalty, was one of unusually intimate domesticity. Following basic repairs, the Prince's rooms were furnished and hung with tapestries and pictures; the Prince's Gallery (i.e. the Queen's Gallery) contained portraits of fourteen admirals by Michael Dahl and Sir Godfrey Kneller, in reference to George's position as Lord High Admiral.

In the last years of his life the Prince was seriously disabled by gout and asthma and appears to have used rooms on the ground floor only. Certainly, this would explain the major works of 1707 that saw the creation of a "new library", for which Grinling Gibbons provided carving and modified three fireplaces. In the same year, orders were issued to John Vanderbank, the Queen's Yeoman Arras Mender, to adapt or provide tapestries for the Prince's Bedchamber and Drawing Room; the former was hung with a newly repaired set entitled *The Children of Israel*, to which three new acquisitions representing *The History of Moses* were soon added. The Drawing Room, already hung with tapestries of hunting scenes to designs by the Flemish artist David Teniers, was provided with suitable pieces to fill the gaps. Of these the *Moses* and *Children* sets have long since disappeared, although some similar to the Teniers tapestries – conceivably those used at Kensington – do still survive in the Royal Collection.

Once Kensington came back into regular use, arrangements had also to be made to accommodate the Queen's household officials, most of whom were newly appointed. Robert Harley, the Lord Treasurer, was also given an apartment. In addition, a large number of more minor officials and, not surprisingly given the poor health of the Queen and her consort, a large staff of doctors, apothecaries and surgeons were also given lodgings. One of the largest apartments was that granted in 1702 to the Duchess of Marlborough who, as the Queen's Groom of the Stole, had both a right and an obligation to be there; it comprised those parts of the Earl of Albemarle's lodgings that had not been taken over by Prince George. It seems, however, that the Duchess rarely used them, preferring the Marlboroughs' lodgings at St James's and, after 1709, at Marlborough House, though she retained them until her celebrated falling-out with the Queen.

"A Palace Royal suitable to so great a Queen"?
Although nothing came of it, it was towards the end of Queen Anne's reign that the possibility of completely rebuilding or replacing Kensington House – thanks once again to its "being so near the town and yet in the country and in the best air in London" – was first considered. In a note or paper prepared by the Office of Works in 1712, probably submitted to Lord Harley, "concerning the building of a Palace ... and for beautifying the Court end of the town", while acknowledging the impracticalities of rebuilding Whitehall, it was noted that, "when the Queen and Parliament shall think fit to build a Palace Royal suitable to so great a Queen and people, the best situation for it is in the High Park, towards the middle

57. The investiture of a Knight of the Garter at Kensington Palace in August 1713, as depicted by Peter Angelis. The ceremony was, and is, usually held at Windsor, but on this occasion the Queen was too ill to travel. The room depicted is probably her Presence Chamber, in part of the house that was rebuilt in the next reign.

of that inclosure which the late Prince George railed in next to Kensington Gardens".

The enclosure in question lay to the east of the existing house, and it was suggested that the new house would face south, be fronted with courtyards and that "there ought to be ground bought in for an avenue, quite down to the river, and that this avenue would point on or near Wimbledon, and that there might be a canal made in it, almost the whole length, from the road without the park ... down to the river".

The old house, it was suggested, could be retained for "the people of the court", but its demolition would allow its replacement better all-round views. Although the paper gives no further details of the design or layout envisaged, it would have been under Wren's control and could have been a finer palace in a finer setting than had been achieved to that date or since. But the note set out no more than a scheme to be considered should the Government "think fit", and it evidently did not, if indeed the Government was even aware of it. Similar ideas, however, prompted partly by the huge potential of Hyde Park as a site and by the limitations of the existing house, were to be put forward in later reigns.

Kensington Gardens and the Orangery

The south gardens

On her first visit to Kensington as Queen, Anne was disappointed by the neglected condition of the gardens, if not immediately by their design and extent. However, although she made very limited use of the house itself in the early years of her reign, the Queen used and greatly enjoyed its surroundings and it is not surprising that she swiftly set about improving them. Precisely what she did in the first years, however, is not particularly clear. In the summer of 1702, Henry Wise submitted a bill for "severall new workes performed for her Majesties Garden att Kensington", including those for a "new Wilderness" and the conversion of a former orchard, but the exact location of these activities is uncertain. Nevertheless, the first major effort must have been concentrated on the south gardens, partly because we know that they were transformed at some stage in Anne's reign, but also because it is difficult to see how else the huge sums and the thousands of bulbs and shaped hollies employed in 1702–03 can be accounted for. Some of the layout of William and Mary's south garden may have been retained, almost certainly including a central north–south path (Dial Walk), axial to the entrance to the King's Gallery range of 1695; "the great circle that was formerly box and is now laid to grass", around which the gravel paths were re-laid in 1702, must also have dated from an earlier scheme: possibly it was one of those shown in the eastern half in fig. 58. In 1705–06 a magnificent "new summer-house" was put up, presumably to Wren's designs, to provide a visual termination and resting place at the south end of Dial Walk (fig. 59).

The Orangery

In William's time the 'greenhouse' facilities at Kensington for overwintering the exotic plants and citrus trees that ornamented the gardens in summer were already inadequate. This must have become more obvious as the gardens expanded, and in 1704 an estimate for a new greenhouse was approved by Queen Anne and the Officers of Works, including Wren and Vanbrugh. Before work began, however, the Queen was persuaded to accept proposals for a more ambitious building, eventually costing almost twice as much. Begun by September 1704 and completed by December of the following year, the resulting structure is architecturally the most accomplished building at Kensington.

Christopher Wren, as the Surveyor, could normally speaking be assumed to have been the Orangery's designer, but its style is quite unlike his own. It does, however, display many features used by Vanbrugh and Hawksmoor, each of whom were in a position to have been involved: Hawksmoor as resident Clerk of Works and Vanbrugh as Wren's principal deputy. In support of Vanbrugh's candidature is the instruction relayed by the Secretary of the Treasury to the Officers of Works that "it is her Majesty's pleasure that the Green House at Kensington be made according to the alteration of the draft proposed by Mr Vanbrugh." Taken literally this would identify him as the architect and, broadly speaking, it is in his style: the semicircular recesses above the cornice at the ends of the main elevation and the banded columns and lunette window at the centre are features he was soon to use at Blenheim Palace. But this cannot be taken as proof, for Vanbrugh's 'proposal' need not have been for a design of his own and motifs of this type were used by both architects. The preferred attribution of the building to Hawksmoor, put forward by Kerry Downes, the principal modern authority on both men, rests partly on the inherent likelihood that, as a proven architect resident at Kensington, he would have been the obvious choice. More important, however, is the design itself. Downes sees in this a strictly geometrical basis in plan and elevation, an attention to and knowledge of detail and the use of "pillars, piers, arches, niches, recessed panels, and pediments ... all used in different patterns and combinations of shape with a thoroughness as well as an economy that are ... typical of Hawksmoor, not Vanbrugh".

On balance, therefore, the actual design of the building is best attributed to Hawksmoor, as Downes suggests. Nevertheless, it seems to have been Vanbrugh's persuasive powers that saw the more elaborate scheme accepted, and credit must be given to the part his own work played in the development of Hawksmoor's style.

49

The interior of the building (fig. 61), originally equipped with underfloor heating, contains a vast central space with a coved ceiling and, at the ends, domed circular compartments lined with eight engaged Corinthian columns, with carved detail by Grinling Gibbons. It was carefully restored in 1898 and its appearance today is much as it would have been when it was built. The level of decoration reflects its intended use, not just as a 'greenhouse' but as a 'summer supper house' and a place for entertainments such as those held by Queen Anne on her birthday. As a result it was also known as the 'Banqueting House', both to contemporaries and to many commentators since.

The Wilderness

In 1704 the Queen revoked her Housekeeper's profitable tenure of land to the north of the house, suggesting that she had another use in mind. Sure enough, in the winter of 1704–05 the full extent of the area now defined by Kensington Palace Gardens to the west, the Bayswater Road to the north and the Broad Walk to the east (fig. 62) was laid out as garden by Henry Wise: divided into four main rectangular sections, further subdivided by right-angled and diagonal rides, it had more the appearance of an ordered, carefully controlled woodland of small trees than what we would normally consider a garden today. It was in fact conceived and referred to as a 'Wilderness', the contemporary English term for a form of garden that had originated in France in the previous century. The south-western quarter, closest to the house and Orangery, however, was an odd one out: here Wise had ingeniously converted a former gravel pit into an elaborate sunken garden, mirrored immediately to the west by a 'Mount' composed not of soil but of trees of carefully graded height (fig. 62). Work in progress was observed by John Bowack, who reported in his *Antiquities of Middlesex* of 1705 that

Her Majesty has been pleased lately to plant near thirty acres more towards the north, separated from the rest only by a stately Green House [the Orangery] not yet finish'd; upon this spot is near 100 men dayly at work, and so great is the Progress they have made, that in less than Nine Months the whole is level'd, laid out and planted and will be very fine.

The issue of Wise's contract for the maintenance of the new garden shows that the Wilderness was completed in the autumn of 1705. It clearly lived up to its promise: the writer and politician Joseph Addison wrote a few years later (particularly of the sunken garden and 'Mount') that he had "never met with any one who had walked in this garden, who was not struck with that part of it". Another contemporary, impressed also by the speed of its creation, acclaimed it as illustrating the "pitch gardening is arriv'd within these twenty or thirty years". No 'bird's-eye' views exist to suggest what it actually looked like, but the essentials of its layout are revealed by a succession of

plans, the earliest of which is by Wise himself (fig. 62).

Wise's plan also illustrates a north–south boundary across Hyde Park, created in 1705 to enclose the 100-acre strip of land closest to the house, foreshadowing the huge eastward extension of the gardens in the next reign (figs. 101, 104) and containing a rectangular tank on the future site of the Round Pond. In Anne's time, however, although managed by Wise, the enclosure was maintained as paddock rather than garden, and by 1713 was being referred to as a 'zoological garden' and stocked with antelopes. The 'bird's-eye' view of c. 1713–14 (fig. 58), the earliest of any value, shows that a small western sector was later separated from the rest of the 100 acres by a wall and a row of trees.

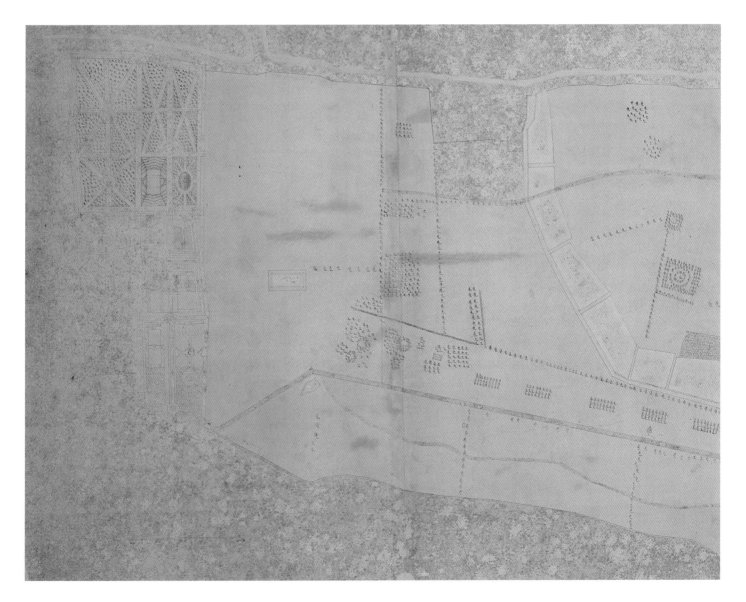

62. *Detail of a plan of Kensington Gardens and Hyde Park made for or by Henry Wise between 1705 and 1725. To the south of the house (shown in faint outline only) is the new garden created in 1702–03 and to the north the vast Wilderness, completed in 1705. To the right (east) of the house and garden area, a large section of Hyde Park had by then been partitioned off; further east still is the series of ponds created by Wise out of the West Bourne stream, later to be remodelled as the Serpentine. William III's lamplit road can be seen traversing the southern part of the park.*

The Royal Palace
KENSINGTON in the reign of GEORGE I 1714–27

George I, Elector of Hanover, arrives in his new kingdom and takes a liking to Kensington; the central part of the house is rebuilt and the interiors decorated by William Kent, after which, its grandeur much increased, the house becomes known as Kensington Palace. A zoo is installed in neighbouring Hyde Park, and plans are made for the expansion of the gardens.

LEFT 63. George I in his coronation robes, from the studio of Sir Godfrey Kneller, 1714.

RIGHT 64. Sophia Dorothea of Celle, married to Elector George in 1682. Her affair with the Swedish courtier Philip von Königsmark led to banishment for life in a remote German castle. She is shown here with her two children, Sophia Dorothea and George (later George II), in a portrait by Jacques Vaillant dated 1690.

The new king

The new king was proclaimed, "mightily to the satisfaction of the people", on the day of Queen Anne's death, and the new reign was celebrated at Kensington with the aid of a bonfire, six barrels of strong beer and over 300 bottles of wine. The banning of strong drink before the following year's anniversary suggests the party was a good one. George himself, however, was in no hurry to take possession, finally arriving at Greenwich in September 1714, with an entourage of more than seventy-five German servants and courtiers, his two Turkish Grooms of the Chamber, Mehmet and Mustapha (fig. 80), his half-sister Madame von Kielmansegge and his mistress, Ehrengard Melusina von der Schulenburg. The former Queen, Sophia Dorothea of Celle, was not among them. Having had an affair in Hanover with a Swedish colonel, Philip von Königsmark, she had been divorced by George and had lived since 1694 in virtual imprisonment in the north German castle of Ahlden, where she remained until her death in 1726. Their children, George Augustus (the future Prince of Wales and later King George II) and his sister, Sophia, although forbidden to see their mother, remained in Germany.

George was not, as is often claimed, a reluctant monarch, but like William before him he saw the position's main advantage as the security it offered to his homeland; also like William, he spent much time in his own country, particularly at Herrenhausen (fig. 65). Neither George's character nor his experience particularly fitted him to be King of England. Although physically courageous, he was shy, not conspicuously intelligent and, although fluent in French and German and competent in Italian, spoke very little English; state papers and other material for his attention (including proposals for improving and decorating his palaces) were, therefore, prepared in French. In common with other rulers and statesmen of his time he also used Latin as a spoken language, famously leading Robert Walpole to 'brush up' his grasp of it, although how he coped with Latin in a German accent is not recorded. George's political experience was also that of virtual absolutism – hardly a good

preparation for dealing with the turbulent English Parliament.

The King's character, un-Englishness and German retinue did nothing for his popularity, and had the Scottish rebellion of 1715–16 in favour of 'James III' taken hold, George would have been in serious danger, as even his own ministers acknowledged. His lack of intellectual interests and the absence of a queen meant that his court had few of the social or intellectual attractions offered, for example, by Charles II's or that of his own son. The King's personal life was overshadowed by the obsessive and mutual hatred between himself and his son, George Augustus, which reached crisis point in 1716–18 and thereafter had a major influence on politics and life at the King's court. George I died in June 1727 at his castle at Osnabrück while on the way to his former wife's long-delayed funeral, and was buried at his successor's request in Hanover.

the new style and its proponents. In May 1718, in one of the great administrative scandals of the century, the aged Wren was dismissed as Surveyor-General and Benson was appointed in his stead. In the event, Benson too was dismissed just a year later, but in that time he had ensured that the new style was applied to the new work at Kensington, although the design itself was probably Campbell's. It was accepted by the King on 19 June 1718.

The new State Apartments

Despite the adverse reports about the state of the building, and whilst the design of its replacement was still being discussed, the King and court took up residence at Kensington in April 1718 and stayed there until early August. A large number of remedial works were put in hand before their arrival, including a temporary reinforcement of the doomed building at the core of the complex, although whether these made it usable is unclear. In any case, its demolition had to await the King's departure. The work was carried out towards the end of the year and at the beginning of 1719, and the shell of the new building was probably complete by the end of that year. The floor levels of the new building were consistent with those of the earlier blocks and so contained a basement or ground floor, a first floor, and a second floor which contained the main rooms and State Apartments. The three most important rooms in the new structure were the King's Drawing Room (overlooking the park), the one that came to be known as the Cupola Room in the centre and, to the west, the Privy Chamber.

Meanwhile, having dismissed his senior subordinates, infuriated his remaining colleagues, shown a habitual economy with the truth and no useful aptitude for the job, Benson had been relieved of the Surveyorship in July 1719. His replacement, under the patronage of Charles Spencer, Earl of Sunderland, who as the new First Lord of the Treasury controlled the appointment, was Sir Thomas Hewett – a man of similar background and architectural tastes to Benson and with little more standing as an architect, but who nevertheless remained in post until his death in 1726. It was through him, therefore, that the King's orders early in 1720, to fit out the interiors of the new rooms, were transmitted: the two lower floors were to be completed in the "cheapest and plainest manner", but the King approved plans to spend more than twice the cost of the other two for the "upper and best storey", in other words the State Apartments. Hewett was, therefore, probably responsible for the structural and architectural elements of the interiors, such as the niches, fireplace and doorcases of the Cupola Room. Assuming that the King used his new rooms while in residence at Kensington between August and October 1721, the other two rooms must also have

71. *William Kent, as portrayed by Bartholomew Dandridge, c. 1736, a few years after the completion of his work at Kensington. Kent was a bon viveur, with a wide circle of friends among the artists and writers of the day and, as his appearance suggests, enjoyed the pleasures of the table.*

been both decorated and furnished, if only provisionally, and some debate remains about which features may survive from this period.

William Kent and the decoration of the King's Apartments

Apart from a few architectural details, surviving work carried out for George I at Kensington is mostly remarkable for its painted decoration. It was originally accompanied by a furnishing programme of almost equal interest, but unfortunately little of this remains *in situ*. This was the work carried out between 1722 and 1727 by William Kent. Although soon to become one of the most prolific and successful Palladian designers – pioneering the extension of the architect's control to the interiors, decoration and furnishing of his buildings – he was then a relatively untried painter with no official position. The boost to his career resulting from his work for the King at Kensington was crucial, therefore, to the future of English design. Kent's first commission there, however, was the cause of one of the greatest controversies of art and patronage of the eighteenth century. The commission would normally have gone to Sir James Thornhill, by virtue of his post as 'Sergeant Painter' (official decorative painter to the King); in addition, Thornhill was much admired by the King and had produced many magnificent works, including the ceiling of the Painted Hall at Greenwich, loaded with loyal tributes to the Hanoverians. Thornhill duly produced designs, a model and an estimate, which the King accepted. But in February 1722, apparently at the invitation of Thomas Coke, the Vice Chamberlain, Kent submitted

72. *The ceiling of the Cupola Room, painted by William Kent in 1722. His receipt of this commission over the head of Sir James Thornhill, the King's official decorative painter, was a subject of great controversy, but was to lead to further commissions for Kent at Kensington in the following years.*

73. *View of the Cupola Room showing William Kent's painted decoration of the walls, completed in 1725, and the fireplace, doorcases and niches installed under Thomas Hewett's direction two years previously. The chandeliers are modern but evoke the design of the lost originals, probably designed by Kent and made by the London firm of Gumley and Moore.*

alternative designs and estimates for £300 and £350 (depending on whether Prussian blue or the more expensive ultramarine, made with crushed lapis lazuli, was to be used), which were presented to the King in March and accepted. Exactly why this happened remains slightly puzzling. Price certainly played a part, as it was the size of Thornhill's estimate that, according to Vertue, led the hard-pressed Vice Chamberlain to approach Kent in the first place; with regard to the final decision, however, it cannot have been crucial as (according to Vanbrugh) Thornhill offered to match his competitor's price as soon as he heard of Kent's selection. Antagonism towards Thornhill within the Office of Works, arising from his attempt at the Surveyorship in 1719 and his later criticism of its officers, might also have been a factor, but neither Hewett's nor the King's appreciation of his talent ever diminished, and in the end the decision was not the officers' to make. More significant was the vigorous promotion of Kent by Lord Burlington, who had met and impressed the King before 1714 and was by now a Privy Councillor, the holder of several government posts and a close associate of the highly influential Vice Chamberlain. But most important of all was Kent's style, which was as in keeping with the Palladian aesthetic as Thornhill's exuberant baroque was not. In any case, swayed by a combination of factors, perhaps including his personal preference, the King approved Kent's proposal, although the Office of Works insisted that his work and its progress should be carefully monitored. In May, by which time the work was half completed, it was duly inspected by a panel of three painters, all of whom were extremely critical – one even suggesting that Kent had cheated on his materials and that the blue colour was "nothing but Prussian blew in which there may be some ultramarine mixt". Nevertheless, in spite of the panel's attempt to get further opinions, the weight of factional and aesthetic opinion was in Kent's favour and by early August he had finished. The work itself (fig. 72), unique among his Kensington ceilings, was entirely of architectural *trompe l'œil*, representing a four-sided coffered cupola of a type well represented in Roman architecture, but with a Garter Star at its apex. The illusionistic effect of the painting was enhanced by the real form of the ceiling, which has steeply curved or coved sides. The decoration of the walls with *trompe l'œil* detailing to the existing pilasters, with swags and military trophies between them, followed in 1723–24; eighteen stools and four large chandeliers were also produced, probably to Kent's designs, by the London firm of Gumley and Moore.

His position bolstered by his success with the Cupola Room, Kent went on to decorate the two other new rooms and seven further spaces at Kensington, four of which included figurative rather than decorative painting. The first to be attended to, in 1722–23, was the King's Drawing Room, where he filled the ceiling oval with a mythological scene in oil on canvas (figs. 74, 75). The fittings of the room, including the plaster coffering that surrounded his painting, were already in place when Kent arrived, but it seems that he was able to replace the chimneypiece to his own design.

FAR LEFT 74. *William Kent's small-scale preparatory drawing for the ceiling of the King's Drawing Room, 1722.*

LEFT 75. *The ceiling of the King's Drawing Room, painted in the late summer of 1722. Jupiter is shown appearing to his lover Semele, who is wreathed in the lightning that was to destroy her. The scene is not presented as if viewed from below, but simply as in an ordinary painting – reflecting William Kent's purely decorative intention, rather than the overpowering three-dimensional effects sought by his baroque precursors. When the canvas was taken down for conservation in 1996 a full-size preliminary sketch for the composition was found on the plaster above it.*

ABOVE LEFT 76. *The ceiling of the Privy Chamber showing Mars and Minerva, god and goddess of war and wisdom, presiding over the arts and sciences, painted by William Kent in 1723.*

ABOVE RIGHT 77. *Detail of the ceiling of the King's Gallery, completed in 1728. The scene shows Odysseus listening to the Sirens, tied to his ship's mast to prevent him from answering their call and destroying himself, while his sailors row on, their ears plugged with wax. The mosaic-like effect between the painted panels was a motif particularly favoured by William Kent.*

RIGHT 78. *The ceiling of the Presence Chamber, for which William Kent was paid in 1724. The central roundel shows the sun god, Apollo, in his chariot.*

ABOVE 79. *Design by William Kent, dated 1725, for the proposed elevation and picture hang of the north wall of the Saloon at Houghton Hall, the Norfolk country house built for Sir Robert Walpole in 1722–35 by Colen Campbell. The picture hang gives a good impression of how Kent's arrangement in the King's Drawing Room at Kensington may once have looked.*

80. *The King's Staircase, enlarged and decorated by William Kent between 1725 and 1727. Among the figures pressing up against the trompe l'œil balustrade are recognizable members of George I's court, including (third arch from left) the King's Polish valet, Christian Ulrich Jorry, and the two Turkish Grooms of the Chamber, Mustapha and Mehmet, who had been with George I since the Vienna campaign of 1686.*

81. *The King's Gallery, looking eastwards. Although it was built for William III, the interior, shown here as restored in 1994, was remodelled and redecorated by William Kent in 1725–27.*

82. *The Queen's Private Dining Room, by James Stephanoff, from W.H. Pyne's* History of the Royal Residences, *1819. The table to the left, composed of a marble top carried by carved and gilded sphinxes, was probably one of a set designed by William Kent for the Cupola Room.*

83. *The north-east corner of the Prince of Wales's Court, as created in the 1720s.*

84. *The main stair of the house forming the north side of the Prince of Wales's Court in the 1720s, most probably intended for Prince Frederick, who became Prince of Wales on George I's death in 1727. The interior, almost certainly designed by William Kent, is shown here as it appeared in 1928, when occupied by the Countess Granville.*

Although this was to have a complex later history, the lower part of his new creation was reinstated in the 1970s and its complete form is known from a number of drawings and engravings. His work extended to "drawing the sides of the Drawinge Room with all the Pictures sketcht in proper Colours designing & drawing the mouldings and ornaments for all the picture frames, glasses etc", a proposal that we can assume was followed, although the drawings are lost (fig. 79). In 1723 Kent also completed the ceiling of the Privy Chamber with a representation of Mars and Minerva, god and goddess of war and wisdom, with symbols of the arts and sciences scattered at their feet (fig. 76). In October of the same year his efforts then turned to the King's Bedchamber, which he provided with a ceiling (destroyed) in the purely decorative 'grotesque' style, shortly to be used also in the Presence Chamber (where his work survives; fig. 78) and in 1724 in the Council Chamber (destroyed). Until 1723 this distinctive style of decoration had appeared in anglicized guise in Tudor and Stuart England, but in its true Renaissance form had been seen only at the Queen's House, Greenwich, designed by Inigo Jones. Its origins, however, lay in ancient Rome, and the name 'grotesque' derived from the decoration of the long-buried rooms or *grotte* ('caves') of the Emperor Nero's ill-fated palace, first discovered in the 1490s. Although Kent had seen antique originals, his interpretation owed more to the works of Raphael and his followers that he had also seen while in Rome. Between 1725 and 1727 Kent painted similar ceilings for the King's Great and Little Closets, both in the south-east pavilion, but unfortunately neither survives.

The most impressive of Kent's rooms – and now, thanks to its restoration in 1994, the one that best demonstrates his intentions – is the King's Gallery, begun in 1725 and finished three years later (fig. 81). Of Wren's interior, completed less than thirty years before, Kent retained only the cornice, dado panelling and William III's wind-dial, replacing the doorcases and chimneypiece to his own designs. The woodwork was painted white and picked out in gold and the walls covered in red damask, making the gallery one of the first examples in England of the white, gold and red formula that was to remain popular for the rest of the century. Kent also designed the window hangings and furniture, including stools, mirrors and marble-topped pier tables, and frames for the pictures – probably selected by the architect but approved in 1727 by the King, the remainder being rehung in other rooms. The most striking feature, however, was the ceiling, which Kent adorned with a series of seven scenes in oil on canvas from the *Odyssey* (fig. 77). The main scenes were linked and surrounded by an elaborate architectural *trompe l'œil* mimicking stucco figures and framing 'relief' panels, painted by an otherwise unknown assistant, Francisco de Valentia.

Kent's last major task was the redecoration of the Great Stair, intended to give the newly enhanced apartments an appropriately impressive introduction. In preparation, the windows in the north wall were blocked to provide a blank surface for painting, and the west wall was rebuilt further out into the courtyard and provided with the existing Venetian window. In the process Jean Tijou's balustrade to the upper landing had to be extended; the eighteenth-century work, conspicuously inferior to the original, can still be identified.

The decorative scheme, consisting of an arcaded gallery running round the upper part of two walls, with figures up against the balustrade between the arches, is something of an unusual one (fig. 80). At first sight it belongs to the baroque tradition of illusionistic decoration to great rooms and stairs, as exemplified in the King's Staircase at Hampton Court by Antonio Verrio, but in fact it remains consistent with Kent's restrained Palladian principles: the painting here does not envelop the entire interior, inviting a real three-dimensional illusion, nor do the figures – selected members of George I's court – stray beyond the confines of their *trompe l'œil* setting.

Artistically, Kent's painted work at Kensington is an important part of his life's work, illustrating the full range of his talents and (as contemporaries were swift to point out) his deficiencies. Combined with his contribution to the furnishing of the rooms and the remainder of their decoration, it gave a consistency between the old and the new parts of the house and a new grandeur to the whole. Nevertheless, there is no overall scheme or logic behind the iconography – at

least in his painted decoration – which might, as was so often the case in royal buildings, have conveyed a political or dynastic message. The explanation probably lies in the work's piecemeal commissioning, a fact which itself reflects the generally declining emphasis on the studied 'alliance of art and power' that had been a sustaining force of the baroque. The choice of some individual subjects and their makers' identity, however, remains a puzzle. In the case of the Cupola Room, the evocation of Imperial Rome certainly offered passive support to the status of the Hanoverian monarchy; to this the painting of the Garter Star at its apex, symbolizing England's most ancient chivalric order, founded in 1348 by Edward III, lent more home-grown credibility to the antiquity, legitimacy and particularly the 'Britishness' of the Hanoverian line – ever a touchy subject. In this case the suggestion may have been made by Robert Walpole, First Lord of the Treasury, who was then in the process of establishing the Order of the Bath as a formalized chivalric order and supporting John Anstis in preparing his two-volume *Register of the Most Noble Order of the Garter* (1724).

The appearance of Mars and Minerva in the Privy Chamber, which might normally have been intended as allegories of the King and Queen, is also puzzling, since an allusion to George's former wife, a wretched exile in Germany, can hardly have been intended. It is possible, therefore, that the reference was to the Prince and Princess of Wales who, in spite of their great breach with the King in 1718, remained his heirs. It has been suggested that the representation of the fatal encounter of Jupiter and Semele in the Drawing Room reflects its supplementary use as a dining room and ballroom, as they were (if by an unusual process) the parents of Bacchus, god of wine and revels. The selection of Odysseus, a mythological royal hero, as a subject for the King's Gallery ceiling needs no special explanation, but it may have been prompted by Kent's close associate Alexander Pope, whose collaborative translation of Homer's epic, for which the artist provided illustrations, was published in 1725. This suggests – not least as Pope was detested by the King – that Kent chose the subject himself, as may also have been the case with the other rooms.

Other works at Kensington

George I's reign saw the transformation not only of the State Apartments and the private apartments of the King and others, but also of the service quarters to the north-west. Between 1724 and 1726 the buildings round what was then called the Kitchen Court (the western of the two to the north of Clock Court; fig. 50) were found to be irredeemably "meane and decaied", and were replaced with the much more substantial ranges that survive today (fig. 94). The old kitchens, occupying the western half of the north range to Clock

Court, were replaced with the existing residential range (fig. 27) – clearly differentiated from the seventeenth-century work by its yellow-grey brick; the new kitchens were placed on the west side of Kitchen Court, with lodgings above. The north side of the new court was occupied by a substantial self-contained house fitted up inside by (or at least in the style of) William Kent (fig. 84). It may have been intended for the Duchess of Kendal, the King's mistress, but was more probably for his grandson, Prince Frederick, who was granted lodgings at the palace in 1727, since when the court has been known as 'The Prince of Wales's'.

Between the new buildings and the back of the Queen's Gallery range lay Green Cloth Court – named after the Board of Greencloth which managed the domestic economy of the royal household and whose Kensington office overlooked it. In 1724 open brick arcades were added to the eastern side of the courtyard, above which (backing on to the Queen's Gallery) a series of rooms was soon added for the Prince of Wales's daughters – hence its renaming as the Princesses' Court.

Kensington Gardens, 1714–27

"Being well satisfied" with his "care and diligence", George I retained Henry Wise in the post of Master Gardener on the terms agreed under Queen Anne, although from 1715 Wise became answerable not to Wren, the Surveyor-General, but to the Surveyor-General of Gardens and Waters, a new post created in that year and awarded to Vanbrugh. By 1716, however, Wise's health was deteriorating and he obtained the King's permission to share the burden of the royal gardens contract; for this he chose Joseph Carpenter, a longstanding colleague and successor

to George London as manager of the Brompton nurseries. When Carpenter died in 1726, his place was filled by Charles Bridgeman, with whom he had worked as long ago as 1709 at Blenheim and who was to become one of the best known and prolific gardeners of the first half of the eighteenth century.

In the early years the King's efforts were focused on the house, but in the mid-1720s his attention turned to the hundred-acre paddock between Kensington Gardens and Hyde Park, which had been enclosed during the previous reign. According to a note of 1731 by Henry Joynes, who had succeeded Hawksmoor as Clerk of Works at Kensington in 1715, the King's "first Intention of the Paddock at Kensington was that of having Animals of different kinds, kept to run and feed at Liberty all over the whole, in the several Lawns, Quarters. & Walks, the Wooded Quarters excepted".

To some extent this was carried out, amplifying what Queen Anne had achieved a few years previously. From the beginning of the reign a number of red deer, elk and horses had wandered at liberty across the plot, watered presumably at the square tank in the middle of it, and been prevented from barking the trees by wooden 'cases' 3 m (9 ft) high. Within a decade, however, more exotic species began to be introduced, effectively creating (in keeping with an ancient kingly tradition) a menagerie such as had most famously been maintained at the Tower of London since the thirteenth century. In January 1725 a tiger was introduced (although housed in a special iron 'den') and in the following year two more arrived and were similarly confined. These were soon joined by two civets, installed in timber cages, and a number of "East Indian" or "outlandish" birds. More surprisingly, at least from today's perspective, was the order issued in May 1725 that "a snailery, and a place for breeding tortices be made at Kensington", the former to be modelled on one the King already had at Richmond. Both were evidently created, as they were improved in the following year and were situated beside the square tank or "bason". What they were for is not explained, but it is hard to believe that the snails were for entertainment; they may, therefore, have been intended for eating.

In 1726 the far-reaching decision was taken almost to double the size of the paddock, by taking in a further acreage of Hyde Park to the east of the old north–south paddock palisade and, at the north end, extending beyond the West Bourne stream. In the summer of 1726 the new ground was enclosed by a brick wall, more than a mile long, and the western end of the King's road diverted to clear the new southern boundary. In the same year, work was under way to impose a formal layout on the newly enlarged acreage, so far occupied by a confused series of grazing areas and copses (fig. 62): trees were planted,

85. Drawing of 1812 showing the water tower built by John Vanbrugh, in this case in his capacity as Surveyor-General of Gardens and Waters, to replace an earlier one in 1716; the design may have been by his associate Henry Joynes. Fed from an adjacent spring by a horse-driven pump, the cistern (in the centre at the top) supplied water to the palace kitchens and service areas, although its poor siting meant that it had to be supplemented in a few years by another one. Until it was demolished in the 1840s, it stood on the site now occupied by No. 3 Palace Green (figs. 94, 107).

rides laid out and the three northern ponds on the course of the West Bourne joined together to create a single lake. In 1727 Bridgeman and Wise submitted an estimate to take the work a stage further "at his Majesty's own direction", which was to include the improvement of the square tank and the creation of the Great Bow – a west-facing semicircle of dense planting embracing it – and the Broad Walk, running north–south across the full width of the gardens and still a major feature of the landscape. Thus, although many of the details of the scheme were created under George II, what were to be the essentials of the gardens' layout at the height of their extent and elaboration were already in place by the end of the reign.

George I at Kensington

On the occasion of his first visit to Kensington, in late September 1714, it was reported that the new King walked "all over the Gardens ... and all over the lodgings, both which he lik't very well". It was an enthusiasm maintained throughout his reign and was reflected by his attention – even if begun out of structural necessity – to the rebuilding and decoration of the State Apartments and his satisfaction with the results. In August 1721 Lady Letchmere, wife of the new owner and occupant of Campden House, wrote that "the court is now in our neighbourhood; they say the King is extremely well pleased with his apartments"; and Vanbrugh wrote to Lord Carlisle in July 1722 that "The king is much pleased with Kensington, and the Easy way of living he is fallen into there". By then the King's intention was clearly to make Kensington one of his most frequented houses, as also observed by Vanbrugh, who, in explaining the rental value of his own lodgings at Kensington to Henry Joynes in 1723, noted that "'tis easy to imagine it may be worth considerably more when the King comes to Spend so much of his time there, as I find 'tis taken for granted he will". Ironically, however, it was the building work George I initiated that so limited his presence there, "for want", as Vanbrugh put it, "of the new Rooms being ready for the King's use". Nevertheless, the King did stay there, in addition to making an uncounted number of day visits, for a total of more than twenty-four months during his thirteen-year reign, the longest continuous periods being in the summers and autumns of 1718, 1721, 1722, 1724 and 1726.

When at Kensington, George I used the apartments, both public and 'privy', which had been created by King William and completed in some details under Queen Anne. The main difference in the use of the royal apartments as a whole was the absence of a queen or consort, which left the Queen's Apartments largely empty until taken over by George's daughter-in-law when she became Queen Caroline in 1727 (see below). In addition, although the Prince and Princess of Wales would under normal circumstances have had apartments at Kensington, and preparations were made for their arrival in 1716, their increasingly hostile relationship with the King meant that they never used them: they went instead to Hampton Court and, after 1718, settled definitively at Leicester House and developed their country residence at Richmond, from where they paid reluctant Sunday visits to 'wait upon' the King at Kensington. Their three young daughters (Anne, Amelia and Caroline), however, whose care and education George had wrested from their parents and confided in the Duchess of Portland, were all lodged at Kensington when he required. The most prominent female member of the household when the King was there was Sophia von Kielmansegge, sometimes assumed to have been his mistress but almost certainly the daughter of the King's father and the Countess von Platen and so his half-sister (his worst enemies said she was both). Although described by Lady Mary Wortley Montagu as having "greater vivacity in conversation than ever I knew in a German of either sex", by the time of George's arrival in England Sophia was best known for her unprepossessing appearance: Robert Walpole's son, Horace, staying at Kensington as a boy, recalled being terrified "at her enormous figure. The fierce black eyes, large and rolling, beneath two lofty arched eyebrows, two acres of cheeks spread with crimson, an ocean of neck that overflowed and was not distinguished from the lower part of her body, and no part restrained by stays".

Exactly where Sophia lived is unclear, but as her rooms had views over the gardens they may have included at least a part of the Queen's Apartments. The King's mistress, Ehrengard von der Schulenburg, whom he created Duchess of Kendal in her own right, also had apartments at Kensington throughout the reign; these presumably overlooked the 'Green Cloth' or Princesses' Court, as the arcaded ground-floor gallery was built there for her convenience in 1725. She was described by Lady Mary, rather more politely than others managed, as "by no means an inviting object", and her attraction was attributed to the fact that she was "duller than the King and consequently did not find that he was so". In 1724 the Comte de Broglie, Louis XV's ambassador, reported that George habitually visited her there "every afternoon between five and eight", and emphasized her huge political influence, based on controlling access to the King and acting as an intermediary between him and his three most important ministers – Robert Walpole, Charles Townshend and Thomas Pelham-Holles, Duke of Newcastle. Walpole himself described the Duchess's position as "in effect, as much Queen of England as any that ever was" and that "he did everything by her".

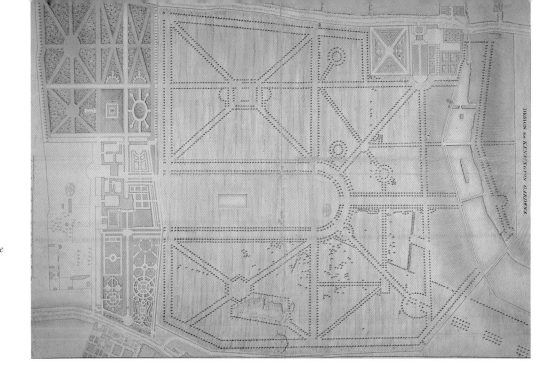

DESIGN for KENSINGTON GARDENS

86. *Plan illustrating an unexecuted scheme for the laying-out of Kensington Gardens, possibly made as early as 1715 but more probably in the mid-1720s. The completed design took in the same area but differed radically in the treatment of the West Bourne ponds and the rectangular 'tank' and in the layout of the main rides and avenues surrounding it.*

87. *Plan of the mid-1720s showing another unexecuted proposal for improvements to the paddock, including a vast geometrical planting in the northern half.*

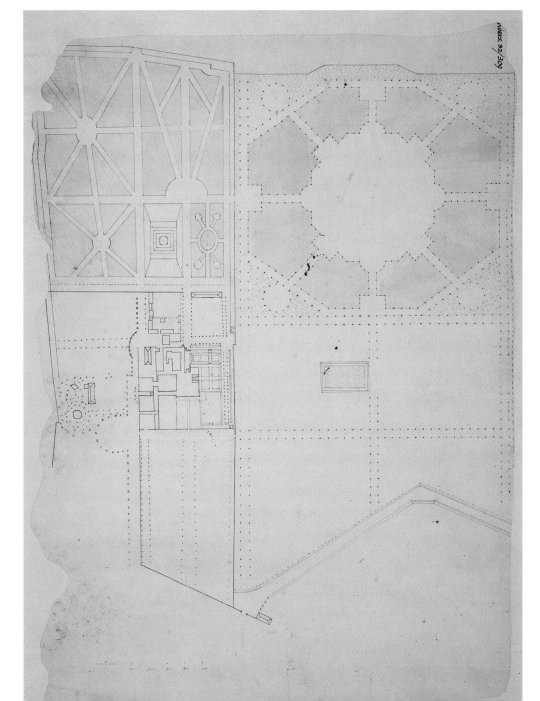

The King also shared Kensington Palace with the traditional complement of household officers and servants. His first three Lord Chamberlains, starting with Charles Talbot, 1st Duke of Shrewsbury, left office before George first used Kensington, but their successors were allocated the usual apartment in the Stone Gallery range. Thomas Coke, who was Vice Chamberlain throughout the reign and who did most of the work, also had lodgings, near the south-west corner of the Princesses' Court; in addition, the King maintained a number of personal servants and associates, largely foreigners, who formed an 'inner court' within the household of considerable social and political significance. Although the major official positions within the household survived the reign and well beyond, the size of the Royal Household as a whole was closely scrutinized and eventually reduced by George I, but as many as 300 individuals – not including his officers' own servants and the outdoor staff – worked at Kensington when the King was there. George was also concerned by expenses related to the numerous private apartments, and as early as April 1715 issued an order that improvements should be charged to the occupant rather than the Crown. From 1719 it was also stipulated that no one should use apartments at Kensington, whatever their entitlement to them, in the King's absence.

For much of the reign the conduct of state business, court routine, the extent of George's public 'visibility' and the character of social life at his palaces were governed by the King's shyness and dislike of ceremony. Although his daily life and calendar was also punctuated, for example, by visits to the theatre, hunting, state events and visits to Germany, his domestic life followed a fairly simple pattern. In keeping with his dislike of ceremony, George abandoned the traditional *levée* or morning meeting with his main household officers. Instead, he remained in his private apartments until midday, attended to, as de Broglie described, "by the Turks, who are his valets de Chambre and who give him everything he wants in private"; these were Mehmet and Mustapha, by then long converted to Christianity, given Hanoverian titles and commemorated in Kent's painting on the Great Stair at Kensington (fig. 80). The King would then emerge from the private apartments, receive ministers and other visitors in an adjoining closet and return after several hours to the Bedchamber for dinner – the largest meal of the day, eaten alone in the mid-afternoon. Later on came his habitual retirement to the Duchess of Kendal's apartments.

Until 1717 the more purely social aspects and functions of court life were left largely to the Prince and Princess of Wales, who enjoyed them – "the pageantry and splendour, the badges and the trappings of royalty" being, as Walpole put it "as pleasing to the son as they were irksome to the father". But in that year increasing differences with his son, and the Prince's dangerous support for political opponents of the King and his government, led George to stage a deliberate reinvigoration of court life. The aim was to refocus attention and loyalty on himself, reaffirm his own position as the source of patronage, advertise his personal support for his ministers and to draw people of influence away from his son's rival court at Leicester House. However unexciting the King may have been himself, his much larger income and his ultimate authority were all on his side, and the stratagem helped pave the way for the partial reconciliation of 1720. The stage for most of this activity in 1717 was St James's Palace and, in the summer, Hampton Court. But in the following year the King was at Kensington solidly from April to August, a period that was to be one of the busiest and socially the most spectacular in its history.

Following the pattern established elsewhere in the previous year, once at Kensington in April 1718 the King began to appear in public much more frequently and initiated a round of extra entertainments. The size of the building meant that the scale and forms of activity possible and appropriate at Hampton Court and St James's could not be fully reproduced at Kensington. Nevertheless, although the King's Apartments did not yet include a Drawing Room as such, in 1718 he did hold regular 'Drawing Rooms' at Kensington, probably in the King's Gallery, which was the largest room and, as a result of Kensington's unusual plan, lay between the outer rooms of the State Apartments and the Bedchamber (fig. 81; inside front cover). Not surprisingly, however, a purpose-built room was included in the scheme for the partial rebuilding of the apartments that the King approved in June of that year, and he made use of it from 1721. Although the 'Drawing Room' was a less formal occasion than it became later in the century, the routine observed was fairly consistent. The King generally sat or stood at one end of the room, part of the company forming a semicircle facing him and conversing in French; on some occasions, particularly towards the end of the reign, George was more mobile, making his way around the 'circle', addressing or cutting the company as he saw fit. Those who attended, other than the higher household officials whose presence was expected, did so primarily to meet or see the King but also to see each other, for the Drawing Room was an important occasion for the gathering of smart society. Attendance was not by invitation, but was open to anyone well enough dressed to be admitted by the footmen at the doors, and was encouraged after April 1718 by opening the road through St James's Park to 'all coaches without distinction'.

In addition to the twice- or thrice-weekly Drawing Room, the King also staged a number of much

larger events, enlivened by music and dancing, which made use of the gardens and Orangery as much as the house itself. The King himself seems to have made particular efforts to be agreeable, a lady participant reporting on one occasion that "the ladies say they never see so much company and every body fine, the King very obliging and in great good humour ... all the garden illuminated and music and dancing in the Green House and the long Gallery".

Particularly lavish festivities were held on 1 August, the official anniversary of the King's accession, and on 28 May, his birthday. Of this occasion the Virginian William Byrd wrote in his diary that he "dressed ... very fine and went to Kensington, being the King's birthday, and about 12 went to Sir Wilfred Lawson's and we went together and found a great crowd in the Gallery, where the King saw company". Later on "the company went into the garden and the dancing was there and the company walked about the garden. About 10'o'clock the fireworks were fired and very fine. The little Princesses danced till 11."

The King spent the next two summers in Hanover and on his return, reconciled to the Prince, largely reverted to his reclusive ways. However, now

equipped with a full set of state rooms, the palace was ready to play a central role in the life of the court when the Prince came to the throne as George II.

GEORGE II and
Queen Caroline 1727–60

Kensington enters its period of greatest use by the monarch, but also its last. George II and Queen Caroline preside over a busy court, enlivened by their differing personalities and interests; the Queen redecorates her apartments and 'discovers' a celebrated set of Holbein drawings, and under her direction Kensington Gardens are extended into Hyde Park, the Serpentine is created and the landscape peopled with buildings and monuments.

LEFT 89. *Portrait of George II in 1759, the last year of his life, by Robert Edge Pine. The buyer of the picture in 1784 reported Pine's explanation that "he had taken the likeness, unseen by the King, as he was speaking to one of his attendants at the top of the great Staircase at Kensington Palace". This is borne out by the representation of William Kent's decoration in the background, although the stone column and balustrade are merely artistic convention. The artist later emigrated to America, where he painted George Washington and other prominent citizens.*

RIGHT 90. *Portrait of Queen Caroline by Joseph Highmore, c. 1735. Much more interested than her husband in the arts and sciences, Caroline was the driving force behind the vast enlargement of Kensington's gardens in the late 1720s and 1730s and a range of changes to the decoration of the palace interiors.*

The King and Queen at Kensington
Royal residence and residents

The new King and Queen moved from Leicester House to Kensington in June 1727, within two weeks of their accession, staying there until September, as St James's Palace was still undergoing improvements begun by George I; moving further afield was not possible as the imminent sitting of Parliament required the King's presence nearby. After this period, however, the King himself spent very little time at Kensington, being either abroad or passing the summers at Hampton Court or, as in 1730, at Windsor. Between 1728 and Queen Caroline's death in 1737, the King spent only one prolonged period at Kensington, from 10 June to 28 October 1734. During the King's summer absences in Hanover in 1729, 1732, 1735 and 1736, however, Kensington was used by the Queen and their children.

Frederick, Prince of Wales, made use of his lodgings at Kensington in 1729 and 1732, and again, briefly, after his marriage to Augusta of Saxe-Gotha in 1736; but after the couple's spectacular falling-out with his parents in 1737, neither lived at Kensington again. One of his brothers, William Augustus, Duke of Cumberland, from the age of ten onwards also had and made use of lodgings at Kensington, at first on or near the north side of the Princesses' Court, and from the early 1730s in the freestanding house to the north built for the Earl of Albemarle in 1696 (fig. 34). (The Duke also had charming rooms at Hampton Court, redecorated by William Kent in 1732, which still survive.)

Four of George II's daughters also continued to use Kensington, at least on an occasional basis – Mary and Louisa until their marriages in 1740 and 1743, and Amelia and Caroline, who never married, during the remainder of the reign.

After the Queen's death the King's use of Kensington changed very considerably. With the Queen's household dispersed and George barely on speaking terms with the Prince and Princess of Wales, the vastness of Hampton Court was no longer essential, and Kensington became viable and attractive as a

base for the whole court. The normal pattern thereafter was for the King to leave St James's for Kensington in April or May and stay there until October or November, during which period excursions were made to Richmond Lodge rather than Hampton Court or Windsor.

In all, George II spent what amounted to nearly eight years at Kensington. While in residence he was accompanied by the usual household officers and, both during and after the Queen's lifetime, by whoever was his current mistress: the first, installed at Kensington by 1728, was Henrietta Howard, Groom of the Bedchamber to Queen Caroline when she was Princess of Wales. Henrietta was falling from favour by the early 1730s, and in 1734 she left the palace for good. She was followed by Mary Scott, the hard-drinking widow of the Earl of Deloraine and governess in the 1730s to Princesses Mary and Louisa. The King's final companion, whom he met in Hanover in 1735, was Amalie Sophie von Walmoden,

RIGHT 91. *Portrait by Charles Jervas, c. 1728, of George II's third son, William Augustus, Duke of Cumberland, who had lodgings at Kensington for most of his life. He is best known as the victor or 'The Butcher' of Culloden, the battle that brought about the final defeat of the Jacobite rebellion of 1745, led by Charles Edward Stuart ('Bonnie Prince Charlie').*

FAR RIGHT 92. *Engraving published in 1738 showing the King in the company of his mistress, Amalie von Walmoden, soon to be created Countess of Yarmouth. After the death in the previous year of the popular Queen Caroline – whose portrait surveys the scene from the back of the room – the King and his mistress were subjected to a certain amount of public ridicule.*

BELOW 93. *View of Kensington Church Street and the church of St Mary Abbots' in about 1750. Kensington's early eighteenth-century expansion from a small village to a substantial town was due largely to the fashionable-ness and custom brought about by the presence of royalty, and the need to provide overflow accommodation for courtiers and servants. Many people also used St Mary's, particularly after the replacement of the medieval church by the one shown here (itself replaced in 1870).*

created Countess of Yarmouth in 1740. Today it might seem slightly strange that these ladies not only shared the same house as the King and Queen but also had adjacent apartments, but in eighteenth-century Europe, as had been the case for centuries, kings' mistresses were normal adjuncts to royal households, even when the royal marriage was genuinely affectionate. Although George's infidelities with these and others offended the Queen's pride – as her friend Lord Hervey put it – on the whole her attitude was one of acceptance and mild relief that she was not the sole object of his attentions.

Buildings and interiors

Building work to the palace under George II was relatively limited. Most attention was focused on the gardens, although the palace's service buildings, drainage system and water supply were modified and improved during this period (fig. 94). The only major operations to the palace itself were the reroofing of the Queen's Gallery in 1728, and in 1731 the replacement and reinforcement of the support structure to the first floor under the State Apartments. Under George II there were also no alterations to the interiors at Kensington on the scale of the previous reign, the most important probably being Queen Caroline's redecoration of her gallery and other rooms, where she had the oak panelling painted white and hung with a new selection of pictures (fig. 2). Although furniture was ordered for the King's personal use and for his State Apartments, further activity was confined to the rearrangement of existing material and pictures, most new orders being for courtiers' rooms and those of the King's children. Until he was accused of over-charging in 1729, the King's main supplier was John Gumley; his partner, James Moore, had died in 1726 and been replaced by William Turing. Gumley and Turing's place was taken by Benjamin Goodison, thereafter the only cabinetmaker to provide material for George II at Kensington, and whose firm remained the Crown's principal supplier well into the reign of George III (1760–1820). Goodison's biggest order was in 1731, when he supplied a long list of furniture, mirrors and other equipment for the use of the young princes and princesses, followed by another large delivery for the apartments of the new Princess of Wales in 1735.

The most interesting developments within the palace were perhaps those associated with the Queen's

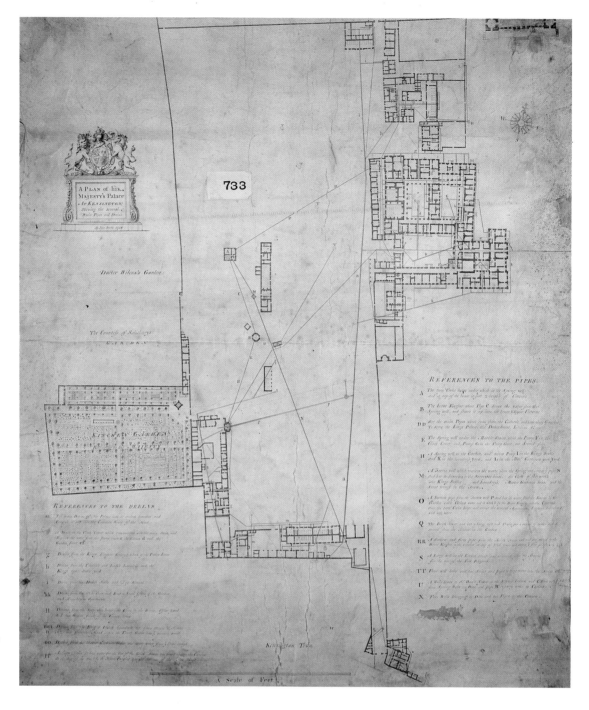

733

94. *Plan of 1754 showing Kensington Palace, its immediate surroundings and associated service buildings. The palace itself and its stables and coach houses, much as left at the end of George I's reign, are shown top right (compare to the plan of 1706–18, fig. 50). To the lower left are the kitchen gardens (fig. 107), in the corner of which stood the square Tudor conduit house (fig. 4). To the right of this is a yard surrounded by buildings, among which, near its southern entrance, is Vanbrugh's water tower (fig. 85). The largest building in the open space above this was the Foot Guards' barracks of the 1690s. The lines identified by letters are drainage routes.*

personal interest in art and, like Mary II, in collecting. These interests were a product of her education and upbringing, firstly at Dresden, where she lived after her mother's second marriage to the Duke of Saxony and became familiar with the celebrated art gallery or *Kunstkammer* founded in the mid-sixteenth century. After her mother's death in 1696 she moved to Berlin under the guardianship of the Elector of Brandenburg, where she met Voltaire and the philosopher and mathematician Gottfried Leibniz, which at least expanded her appreciation of intellectual activity. From 1705, as daughter-in-law of Elector George of Hanover, she became familiar with the collection of curiosities and rarities (known in German since the sixteenth century as a *Wunderkammer*) assembled at

Herrenhausen by her grandmother-in-law, the Electress Sophia. At Kensington, Caroline was not slow to take advantage of her position and the wealth of material already in royal possession, and installed her own *Wunderkammer* in the lower room of the north-east pavilion, which had been George I's library. Among the things displayed there, according to Walpole's handwritten annotations to W. Bathoe's *Catalogue* of the pictures at Kensington published in 1758, were "flaggons of ivory carved", branches of coral set in gilt mounts, a "crystal shell and triton set with jewels", gems, medals and natural curiosities. Some of the material had been inherited, particularly from the collections of Charles I and Mary II, but Caroline certainly added new items herself. Another

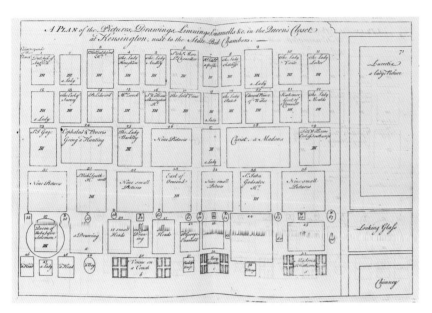

ABOVE LEFT 95. *Diagram included in the catalogue published in 1758 by the engraver and antiquary George Vertue, showing the arrangement of pictures in the 'Queen's Closet' at Kensington as found in 1743.*

ABOVE RIGHT 96. *Giltwood chandelier made c. 1730, one of four hung in the Queen's Gallery by Queen Caroline (see fig. 2). It now hangs in the Queen's Drawing Room.*

RIGHT 97. *Drawing by Hans Holbein of William Reskimer, a Page of the Chamber to Henry VIII from 1525. This was among those 'found' at Kensington by Queen Caroline, and is shown by Vertue's diagram to have been displayed there in 1743 (fig. 95).*

inventory, made on behalf of the Housekeeper in the mid-eighteenth century, records that the room contained a series of "very fine curious cabinets", one of which was accompanied by written instructions for opening it without disturbing the contents. The whole was presided over by a portrait of Robert Boyle, long dead by Caroline's time but whom she presumably recognized as one of the country's greatest scientists. The collection remained at Kensington until it was moved to Windsor in 1764, and the books it displaced joined those in the new library that Caroline had built at St James's Palace by William Kent.

Queen Caroline also had a German-inspired enthusiasm for lineage and genealogy, translated in England into a passion for its history and representations of its great men, its monarchs and their consorts. In the grounds of Richmond Lodge she created a 'Hermitage', peopled with busts of British philosophers and scientists, and began another building displaying statues of English kings from the Conquest onwards. At Kensington this aspect of her interests, combined with that for art itself, found expression in the five pictures of English sovereigns and their consorts, alongside their continental relatives, that she selected for the Queen's Gallery (fig. 2). Equally importantly, it led her to display a series of drawings by Hans Holbein, the celebrated artist of the time of Henry VIII, which Horace Walpole tells us that she found in "a bureau in his Majesty's Great Closet". Bound together with other Old Master drawings, this was probably the "greate Booke of Pictures done by Haunce Holbyn" mentioned in 1590 as a former possession of Edward VI (1547–53), which had

returned to royal ownership in the reign of Charles II and probably been brought to Kensington by William III. The Queen had the volume unbound, the drawings framed and taken briefly to Richmond Lodge; they were then displayed at Kensington in one of the small second-floor rooms Queen Anne had added to the back of the King's Gallery. Here they were observed by Walpole, in what he considered "a very

ABOVE LEFT 98. *Giorgio Vasari's* Venus and Cupid, *the subject of a famous altercation between George II and Queen Caroline at Kensington. The painting was based on a cartoon by Michelangelo, whom the artist much admired and claimed as his tutor.*

ABOVE RIGHT 99. *Portrait of Lord Hervey by Jean Baptiste van Loo, c. 1740–41. Hervey was a prominent figure at the court of George II and Queen Caroline, and his memoirs, although biased and not wholly reliable, provide a uniquely important depiction of the life and politics of their court.*

improper place" for their display, "some hanging against the light, or with scarce any, and some so high as not to be discernible".

The King did not share such interests. Walpole tells us that "he used often to brag of the contempt he had for books and letters" and "to say how much he hated all that stuff from infancy" – although perhaps as much to nettle the Queen as out of conviction.

The court at Kensington, 1727–60

For court life under George II and Queen Caroline, at Kensington and elsewhere, we depend on *Some Materials towards Memoirs of the Reign of King George II*, by John, Lord Hervey, Vice Chamberlain from 1730 to 1740, which begin in 1733 and end with an account of Queen Caroline's death in 1737. Although Hervey was as respectable a family man as most of his contemporaries, his effeminate looks and manner earned him the scorn of many contemporaries – Alexander Pope referred to him as that "amphibious thing" who "now trips like a lady and struts like a Lord" (fig. 99), and, worse still, Lady Mary Wortley Montagu described the human family as consisting of "men, women and Herveys".

The routine of the court and the King's daily life was not vastly different from that under George I, and the 'Drawing Room', held two or three times a week, remained the main public event. The oft-cited Kensington incident of October 1742, provoked when a lady of the court pulled away the Countess Deloraine's chair as she was sitting down, no doubt took place on one of these occasions: annoyed that the King found this funny, the Countess did the same

thing to him, but "alas", as Walpole tells us, "the monarch, like Louis XIV is mortal in that part that touched the ground and was so hurt and so angry that the Countess is disgraced and her German rival [Lady Yarmouth] remains in sole and quite possession".

Another celebrated incident, illustrating the King's character and a deterioration in his relationship with the Queen, involved the picture hang in the King's Drawing Room, which she (as Hervey saw it) had improved during one of his absences abroad. The King was furious and ordered the previous selection to be put back. Referring to Vasari's *Venus and Cupid*, Hervey then asked the King whether he would "have the gigantic fat Venus restored too?", and having received his emphatic confirmation, set down that he "thought, though he did not dare say, that, if His Majesty had liked his fat Venus as well as he used to do, there would have been none of these disputations ...". Hervey's account of what happened next offers another vignette of George's boorish behaviour: just after the King's answer had been passed on to Queen Caroline, the King came in and

stayed about five minutes in the gallery; snubbed the Queen, who was drinking chocolate, for being always stuffing, the Princess Emily [Amelia] for not hearing him, the Princess Caroline for being grown fat, the Duke [of Cumberland] for standing awkwardly, Lord Hervey for not knowing what relation the Prince of Sultzbach was to the Elector Palatine, and then carried the Queen to walk, and be resnubbed, in the garden.

100. *Charles Bridgeman, Royal Gardener between 1728 and 1738, was responsible for designing and managing the vast expansion of Kensington Gardens into Hyde Park. Pencil sketch by Sir James Thornhill.*

Nevertheless, the court's life at Kensington had its lighter side and fair share of festivities. An example was that of August 1743 to celebrate the capture of Valenciennes, in the same campaign of the War of the Austrian Succession as the Battle of Dettingen in which the King had fought himself (the last reigning English monarch to do so). On this occasion the whole palace and the surrounding trees were lit up with candles, and a newspaper reported that "Musick serenaded the company present, who were regaled with a cold collation on the stone pavement in front of the palace. Those who had the pleasure to partake of this exhilarating repast acknowledge the excellence of design and the happiness of its execution".

One of the more extraordinary events to take place at Kensington in this period, but also one of some international importance, was the visit in the summer of 1734 of the king, queen and a number of chiefs of the Creek tribe of Native Americans. They had been brought over by James Oglethorpe, who had founded Savannah and the colony of Georgia in the King's name in 1732–33, a colony that depended on the Creeks' allegiance for security against the Spaniards of neighbouring Florida. Having been persuaded by Oglethorpe to wear more than the "covering around their Waste, the rest of the body being naked", but still with "their faces ... variously painted after their Country['s] manner, some half black, others triangular, and others with bearded arrows instead of whiskers", they were received in the Presence Chamber: speeches of mutual respect were made and the visitors then proceeded to the Queen's Apartments and exchanged addresses with Queen Caroline, seated on a throne in the 'Great Gallery'.

After the Queen's death at St James's Palace in 1737, life at Kensington lost much of its glitter, despite the fact that the King's use of Kensington increased. Horace Walpole explained this in the following terms: "where the Monarch is old, the courtiers are seldom young; they sun themselves in a window, like flies in autumn, past even buzzing, and to be swept away in the first hurricanes of a new reign". He was no more generous in his account of the King's death at Kensington, which took place in his water closet –

101. *Plan made for Charles Bridgeman in about 1733, showing Kensington Gardens on the completion of the work begun in 1725. Some alterations inherited from George I had by then also been made to the layout of the gardens near the palace, including the replacement of the south gardens by lawn, but the main achievement of these years was the vast eastward expansion into Hyde Park. Most of the layout has since been lost, with the exception of some rides, the Serpentine (right), the 'Round Pond' and the planting of the 'Great Bow' around it. To the far right can be seen the new boundary of the gardens with the remainder of the park, 'fortified' with mock bastions.*

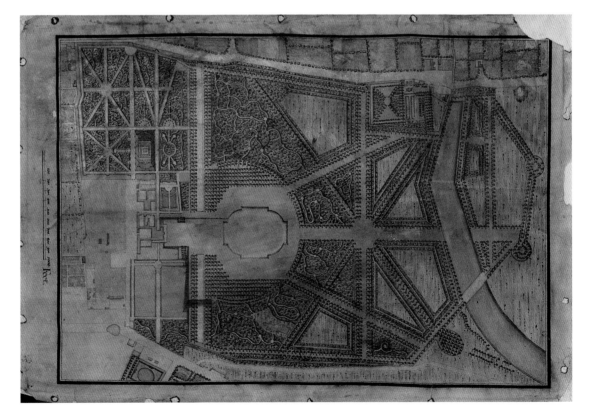

an English invention of the sixteenth century in use at the palace since the reign of King William. In a letter to George Montagu, he wrote that the King

> went to bed well last night, rose at six this morning as usual ... and called for his chocolate. A little after seven, he went into the water-closet; the German valet de Chambre heard a noise, listened, heard something like a groan, ran in, and found the hero of Oudenarde and Dettingen on the floor, with a gash on his right temple, by falling against the corner of a bureau. He tried to speak, could not, and expired.

The King had in fact been struck down by a heart attack – the last of four sovereigns to die in the palace.

Kensington Gardens transformed

As in the decoration of the palace, the major impetus for improvements to the gardens came not from the King but from the Queen, whose interest in gardens had long been nurtured in Germany, particularly at Herrenhausen. The work was supervised at first by Bridgeman and Wise, but after Wise's death in 1728 by Bridgeman and Charles Withers, whose title was 'Surveyor of Woods and Forests', although he was effectively Bridgeman's deputy.

The first task was to complete the work ordered by George I, including the conversion of the West Bourne ponds within the newly extended paddock – soon to become garden – into a single lake, and the conversion of the rectangular pond to the east of the palace to create the existing Round Pond. More ambitious plans then followed, the end results of which are best illustrated by the plans made by Bridgeman in 1733 and the cartographer John Rocque in the 1736 (figs. 101, 104). As Bridgeman himself put it in 1731: "Their present majesties, altering the first design, have made the whole into a garden by increasing the walking parts thereof, by planting espaliers and sowing wood to enclose the several paddock quarters, which by the first design was to have laid wild and open, and also by several other improvements and alterations".

Apart from work in the new gardens, Bridgeman was also ordered by the Queen to make major changes to the old, the most drastic being that the gardens "from the orangery down to the southern extent next the town" should be completely swept away and made into lawn; in the fashion of the time – promoted by Kent and Bridgeman among others – the grass now came right up to the walls of the house itself (figs. 105, 106). On the east side this allowed an uninterrupted view over the developing landscape, its layout centred on, and best admired from, the King's Drawing Room. Henry Wise's Wilderness to the north of the palace was retained, but altered with the cutting of 'serpentine' paths through the thickly planted areas between the main walks (compare figs. 62 and 101).

In the layout of the new gardens, the first achievement, completed by the end of 1728, was the Grand

Walk, running north–south across the former park, which survives today as the Broad Walk. This was followed by the north and south boundary walks, the great circular lawn around the Great Basin and the east boundary walk, all completed by the middle of 1729. The various cross and diagonal walks were finished in 1730, the great east–west middle avenue and the small serpentine walks ordered by the Queen in 1731, and the planting of the area between the new lake and the boundary with Hyde Park was completed. At the same time, the eastern and south-eastern stretches of the new brick wall were augmented with a ditch, faced on the west side with a retaining new wall with a terrace behind it, and fronted by "two circular platforms joining to the said terraces". These semi-circular 'bastions' – the northern two of which can still be traced in the much-altered landscape of Hyde Park today – were the product of a late seventeenth- and eighteenth-century fashion for surrounding houses and gardens with military-style ditches and ramparts. In some cases these had a real purpose, but more usually they were intended to proclaim the martial credentials of their owners. Their use at Kensington may have appealed personally to George II, ever the frustrated soldier and very proud of his military record, and would certainly have made a good vantage point and backdrop for the drill sessions that were then held regularly in Hyde Park.

By this stage Kensington Gardens proper had taken on the form retained until beyond 1760, but one major change remained to be completed in the adjacent park: this was the joining-up of the six ponds on the course of the West Bourne on the Hyde Park side of the boundary and their linking to the lake within the gardens of 1727–30, under the supervision of Charles Withers. This involved creating a massive dam, which still retains the lower end of the lake and its associated sluices, and was completed by the summer of 1731. According to a notice in a September 1730 edition of *Read's Weekly Journal*, and a similar one in the *London Journal*, this work was to be accompanied by the building of "a royal mansion in Hide Park", to be designed by Thomas Ripley, successor to John Vanbrugh as Comptroller of Works. This proposal is not known from any other source, but the rumour or information picked up by the press was in keeping with the current view, as expressed by another journalist in 1731, that the park "was possessed of every beauty and convenience which might be required in the situation of the palace of the British King". Similar suggestions were to be made at various points over the next hundred years.

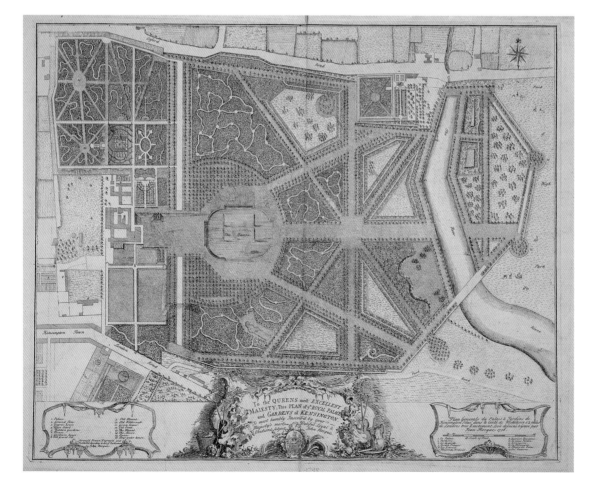

104. *John Rocque's 'Plan of the Palace Gardens and Town of Kensington', published in 1736 when the gardens were at the height of their splendour.*

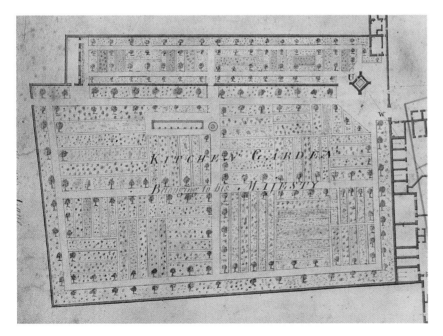

TOP 105. *View of the palace from the south-east, published in 1746. To the left, overlooked by the King's Gallery range, is the vast lawn that, at Queen Caroline's request, replaced the elaborate gardens laid out under William III and Queen Anne. The north–south path remains today; the east–west route was moved northwards towards the palace after 1850. To the right is part of the avenue lining the Broad Walk.*

MIDDLE 106. *The East Front of Kensington Palace viewed from beyond the Great Basin (the Round Pond) in 1736. To the right and left are some of the trees planted in the 1720s, and behind them can be seen the high hedges that by then flanked Dial Walk (left) and for a short time screened the garden to the south of the Orangery. Entry to the gardens was open to anyone, such as those shown enjoying them here, whose dress and appearance met the approval of the gatekeepers.*

BOTTOM 107. *Detail from the 'drainage' plan of 1754 (fig. 94), showing the kitchen gardens or "forcing ground" at Kensington, which lay to the south-west of the palace until replaced by barracks in the 1840s. They were managed by the Master Gardener, whose responsibilities in the mid-eighteenth century included producing "varietys of eatables most proper for his Majesty's use" at Kensington and elsewhere.*

Still to be added within the gardens was the conical mound of earth or 'Mount', created in 1731–32 at the south-eastern angle of their new boundary. In the following year a 'seat' designed by William Kent (fig. 103) was built on it. The gardens as completed served an important function as a fine-weather venue for festivities otherwise held wholly or partly inside the palace, as well as insulating the palace from the outside world, but above all they were invaluable as a place of recreation. George II, although no great gardener, certainly enjoyed them, regularly riding or walking there, even, according to Hervey, "in frost and snow which, before it affected their Majesties, had made all their attendants sick". Public admission was controlled by gatekeepers, but only to the extent that they excluded people of un-genteel appearance, although not always with great perspicacity: in 1738 the King himself was accosted by a cross-dressing political maniac, after which, for a while, military patrols searched the gardens every night. Those admitted, however, certainly appreciated the gardens, at this time at the very height of their splendour. Verses published in the *Gentleman's Magazine* in 1733, indulging in a pastoral orgy of praise for Queen Caroline, the gardens and their unaffected Englishness, give us a flavour of the impression they made:

> At ev'ry step, new scenes of beauty rise,
> Here, well judg'd vistos meet th'admiring eyes:
> A river there waves thro' the happy land,
> And ebbs and flows, at Caroline's command.
> No costly fountains, with proud vigour rise,
> Nor with their foaming waters lash the skies;
> To such false pride, be none but Louis prone,
> All she lays out in pleasure is her own.

Kensington
PALACE 1760–1837

George III forsakes Kensington for Buckingham House; the State Apartments, unused, are visited by the public but many works of art are removed to other royal residences. After 1800 the maze of apartments once used by courtiers and royal children is occupied by senior members of the royal family; the future Queen Victoria is born there in 1819, lives there as a child and there receives the news of her accession in 1837.

LEFT 108. The Duchess of Kent and her daughter, Princess Victoria, by Henry Bone after Sir William Beechey (1821). The Princess is holding a miniature of her father, who had died in the previous year.

BELOW 109. George III, Queen Charlotte and their Six Eldest Children by Johann Zoffany, 1770. Although the King and Queen made no use of Kensington themselves, three of their children made it their home in the early nineteenth century, including Edward, later Duke of Kent (third from left), the father of Queen Victoria.

The palace neglected, 1760–1805

George III

At the death of Frederick, Prince of Wales in 1751, his eldest son, George William Frederick, the new Prince of Wales, was granted the use of his father's long-disused apartments at Kensington, but neither then nor during his reign did George III show any inclination to live there. Exactly why is unknown, but possibly the palace retained unpleasant associations arising from his parents' repudiation of it following their appalling quarrel with George II and Queen Caroline in 1735. In any case, on George II's decision to provide his eighteen-year-old grandson with his own establishment, the Prince confided to Walpole that he "desired to be excused living at Kensington"; he remained instead at Savile House in Leicester Square, leased for his use since 1751, although with a newly constituted household.

Once on the throne, George had the full use of St James's Palace but, for reasons similar to those of his predecessors, he still required another house a little

further out of town. Having ruled out Kensington, he considered the lease of Wanstead House in Essex, but in 1761, following his marriage to Charlotte of Mecklenburg-Strelitz, he bought Buckingham House, a fine red-brick building of 1705 designed by William Winde and with gardens by Henry Wise. Following a process reminiscent of William III's purchase of Nottingham House, George thereby provided himself with what he called "a retreat not a palace", maintaining St James's as the sovereign's official home, as it remains today. In 1775, Buckingham House was settled by Act of Parliament on Queen Charlotte. This was in exchange for the old Somerset House (about to be rebuilt in its present form). As a result, Buckingham House became known as the Queen's House, until it came to be called a palace in the next reign.

As far as the King was concerned these arrangements were perfectly adequate, but many of his subjects, conscious that the growing importance of Britain and its King on the world stage required a great palace in the capital, thought differently. Various schemes were produced to put things right; most of these would have condemned Kensington Palace to destruction, including the far-sighted ideas for the replanning of London published by the architect John Gwynn in 1766, according to which the existing palace would have been removed and replaced by a much grander structure in the middle of Hyde Park (fig. 111). Other schemes for a great palace in the park were dreamed up on their own initiatives by the young John Soane and James Wyatt, in the late 1770s and 1798 respectively (fig. 112). Some new work was actually carried out at other sites, however, including the construction of a new house near the castle at Windsor, but the most important was at Kew, where until the end of the eighteenth century George used the small house remodelled by his father and the seventeenth-century 'Dutch House' (fig. 8). Here, in a move that could have fundamentally altered the future of other royal residences every bit as much as a new palace in London, Wyatt was privately commissioned to supplant the older buildings with a vast gothick palace. (In the event, however, it was never completed, and was

and 1819 the internal walls and floors of the south-east pavilion, sandwiched between the King's Drawing Room and the King's Gallery range, were also rebuilt, although the interiors were only finished, for another purpose, in the 1830s.

One substantial piece of work was carried out to the State Apartments during this period, however – the rebuilding in 1811 of the north-east pavilion. This had contained King William's Council Chamber and been part of Wren's first campaign of 1689, but by 1810, as described by the Duke of Kent, it was in a "ruinous" and "dangerous" state. When viewed from the outside, minor differences in detailing and the colour of its brickwork clearly distinguish it from the earlier fabric.

Royal residence again, 1805–37

The palace and its upkeep

The decades of near-abandonment came to an end in the opening years of the nineteenth century when the palace was brought back into royal use for three of the numerous children of George III: Edward, Duke of Kent (1767–1820), Augustus Frederick, Duke of Sussex (1773–1843) and Princess Sophia (1777–1848). In addition, from 1808 until 1814 the spurned Princess of Wales, Caroline of Brunswick (fig. 115), had apartments at Kensington where she held loud and mildly disreputable parties; it was there that her daughter, Princess Charlotte, was allowed to visit her under the strict terms of access set down by the Prince Regent. In the last years of George III's life and in the next two reigns, however, the future of the palace was once again threatened by schemes for a new building in Hyde Park. The earlier projects were prompted by the concerns of George's heir, first as Prince Regent and then as King George IV, about the lack of a London palace that fitted his grandiose ideas. One such scheme, prepared in 1818 by David Laing, a former pupil of John Soane's, may at least have been presented to the Prince, as the drawing remains in

114. Drawing produced by the architect David Laing in 1818 for the building of a new palace in Hyde Park, reflecting the continued perception, unresolved until the rebuilding of Buckingham House after 1825, that the King should be provided with a suitably dignified palace in the capital. As with earlier Hyde Park schemes, Kensington Palace would probably have been swept away.

the Royal Library (fig. 114). Another, drawn up in 1825 at the instigation of Charles Arbuthnot, Commissioner for Woods and Forests, by James Wyatt's son Philip, certainly caught his eye, as the Commissioner's wife reported that the King was "madly eager" for it, although he was also aware of the hopelessness of getting his ministers' agreement. The King's decision in 1826 to rebuild Buckingham House as a gigantic palace put paid to the real chances of any further schemes, although ironically enthusiasm was rekindled by the parliamentary debate that led to its financing. Soane himself continued to offer designs for a new palace to the reading public and his lecture audiences, although more for amusement and instruction than with any hope of seeing one built.

At a more mundane level, the period also saw further alterations in the personnel and management of royal buildings and their upkeep, which shifted the administrative and financial responsibility for Kensington's future. Following the death in 1813 of William Chambers's successor, James Wyatt, professional responsibility for Crown buildings was apportioned to three architects 'attached' to the Office of Works – the first appointees being John Nash, Robert Smirke and John Soane. The Surveyorship, now a purely administrative post, was given to an ex-soldier and courtier, Charles Stephenson. Kensington, along with St James's Palace, fell to Nash, although his greatest efforts were to be concentrated at Buckingham Palace and, as the Prince Regent's private employee, at Brighton Pavilion. More changes came in 1832 with the amalgamation of the Office of Works and another ancient department, that of Woods and Forests, and the transferral of the joint body's control to three Commissioners of Woods and Work; until 1851 the first Commissioner (as it happened, always a peer) had an *ex officio* seat in Parliament. Changes were also afoot on the financial front. Until 1831, funds for maintenance and building work on the King's behalf at Kensington and other royal residences had been drawn from the Civil List. In that year, following the death of the hugely extravagant George IV, the list payment was reduced by more than half and the responsibility transferred to Parliament; thereafter an annual sum, based on the Surveyor's estimates, was voted by Parliament for the maintenance of a carefully drawn up list of sites and buildings. In the 'Vote' lies the origin of today's system of 'Grant in Aid', a contribution to the upkeep of buildings used for official purposes by the Head of State.

The Kents and their daughter

The first of the new royal occupants at Kensington was Edward Augustus, the King's fourth son, created Duke of Kent in 1799. In 1798 George III ordered that the King's Private Apartments, extending over two floors underneath the State Apartments in the south-

east corner of the palace, should be made ready for Edward's use. The initial requirement that they should simply be "fitted up" and "painted and whitewashed" was wildly optimistic, as the rooms had been empty, apart from "old and decayed furniture", since 1760 and a considerable amount of work was needed. As a result, from 1798, and then with renewed vigour after his return from a disastrous term as Governor of Gibraltar in 1804, the Duke embarked upon a programme of building and decoration kept up until his death. Driven by a keen and knowledgeable attention to detail and a military-style desire for efficiency and practicality, he bombarded the Clerk of Works, John Yenn, and his masters with endless demands for improvements. Matters were not helped by Wyatt's hopeless inefficiency, and the tensions between the Duke, the architect, the Clerk of Works and the Treasury were very great. The result, by the end of the Duke's life in 1819, was a transformation of the rooms in question – and a gigantic final bill, four times the sum spent on the Duke of Sussex's apartments (see below).

The largest alteration to the planning of the palace in the nineteenth century, and the most prominent survival today, followed from the rearrangement of the entrance to the Duke's apartments. These had originally been approached along the Stone Gallery and past the King's Stair but, with the installation of the Duke of Sussex at the far end of the Stone Gallery in 1806, a more direct entrance was needed, and a new porch opening on to Clock Court was soon created. This opened into a new single-storey hall, on the site of Wren's gallery, leading to the foot of what a contemporary newspaper account described as a "grand staircase ... of magnificent appearance ... composed of a double flight to one grand landing", presumably designed by Wyatt. The correspondent also much admired the "Grecian" detailing of the iron balustrade, the ceiling and the furniture in the rooms beyond, together with a number of magnificent *scagliola* tables the Duke had imported from Rome.

After a brief period in Brussels taking refuge from his creditors, the Duke attempted to return to his eccentric bachelor existence at Kensington, but this was to come to an end following the death in 1817 of Princess Charlotte, daughter of the Prince Regent and the estranged Queen Caroline. In the absence of any other legitimate children, the succession now lay with George's brother, the Duke of York, married to a Prussian princess, and any children he might have. Should the Yorks have remained childless, the throne would have passed to the other brothers in order of seniority. In the event, George IV was succeeded not by the Duke of York, who died in 1827, but by William, Duke of Clarence who ruled as William IV (1830–37). Meanwhile, however, the bachelor dukes had come under pressure to marry, and the Duke of Kent, not entirely unswayed by the promise of a larger income, decided to comply. His choice was Victoria, daughter of the Duke of Saxe-Coburg-Saalfeld, widow of the Prince of Leiningen-Dachsburg-Hardenburg and Regent of the Principality; she was also the sister of Prince Leopold, husband of the late Princess Charlotte, elected first King of the Belgians in 1830. (Equally significantly, her other brother, Ernest, the reigning Duke of Saxe-Coburg and Gotha, was the father of Prince Albert, future husband of Queen Victoria.) Married first at Coburg, they went through

TOP 117. *View of the west side of Kensington Palace from Palace Green in 1826, by the architect and antiquarian John Buckler, showing the King's Gallery range to the right and the newly rebuilt porte-cochère to the left. At this period, although no longer used by the monarch, the palace once again had a large number of royal residents, including the young Princess Victoria and her mother.*

ABOVE 118. *Stair built for the Duke of Kent in about 1807, linking the new entrance to Clock Court to the main rooms of his apartment.*

a second ceremony, jointly with the Duke of Clarence and Princess Adelaide of Saxe-Meiningen, at the Dutch House at Kew (fig. 8), in the presence of the dukes' mother, Queen Charlotte, who was too ill to move.

After a short stay at Kensington, the Duke of Kent's debts forced a brief retirement to the Duchess's ancestral seat at Amorbach but, determined that their child should be born English, they returned in 1819 in time for the birth of their daughter at Kensington Palace on 24 May. Precisely where this took place is unknown, although tradition as early as the 1850s placed it in the North Drawing Room; certainly the room was on this floor, as the Duchess's encroachment on the State Apartments took place only in the 1830s. The Princess was christened in the Cupola Room, using what the diarist and eyewitness Charles Greville called the "gold font" – presumably the magnificent silver-gilt item made for Charles II in 1660 and now displayed in the Jewel House at the Tower of London.

Nevertheless, loathing the Duchess, suspicious of the Duke and mindful of the recent death of his own daughter, the Prince Regent insisted on a simple, private occasion. At the ceremony itself, refusing to allow either Charlotte or Augusta to be included among her names, he supported the Duke's suggestion of Alexandrina (after her godfather Alexander I, Tsar of Russia) as the first. Countering the Duke's "urgently" proposed choice of Elizabeth, he suggested that as her second name she should take her mother's – Victoria.

Eight months later, in January 1820, the Duke died unexpectedly at the rented house in Sidmouth to which, for reasons of economy, he had taken his family for the winter. The return of his wife and daughter, now literally penniless, to Kensington, and the refurnishing of their apartments (the Duke's furniture having become the property of his creditors), was only possible through the generosity of the Duchess's brother, Leopold. There, for the next twelve years or so, the young Princess was brought up. According to her own recollection in 1872, her first memories were of being at Kensington, crawling on a yellow carpet and being told that if she cried and was naughty her "Uncle Sussex" would hear and punish her – for which reason, she wrote, "I always screamed when I saw him." Until the age of five the Princess was in the charge of her nurse, Mrs Brock, by whom she later recalled she had been "very much indulged"; her care was then taken on by Louise Lehzen (fig. 122), already part of the household as governess to Princess Feodora, the Duchess's daughter by her first marriage. Not surprisingly, Lehzen was a major influence on the younger Princess's development and remained a crucial confidante until the latter's marriage in 1840. By the time the Princess was ten, the governess was managing a daily routine with the aid of professional tutors; by the late 1820s, with the aid of a resident Principal Master, this involved lessons from 9.30 in the morning until 6.00 in the evening, with a two-hour interval in the middle of the day. Lehzen herself taught the Princess history, and it was she who engineered Victoria's realization, in the course of a lesson at Kensington, that she would one day be queen – the occasion of her famous declaration "I will be good." The domestic routine seems to have been kept as unceremonial as possible, Queen Victoria later recalling, "We lived in a very simple plain manner ... breakfast was at half past eight, luncheon at half past one, dinner at seven – to which I came generally (when it was no regular large dinner party) – eating my bread and milk out of a small silver basin."

But life at Kensington was not all lessons and routine. Although by normal standards the Princess had a lonely childhood, she spent and enjoyed a great deal of time with her older half-sister, Feodora, until 1828 when the latter was married, in the Duchess's apartments, to a German prince. Lehzen too was prepared to play with Victoria, for example helping her to dress her collection of 132 dolls (fig. 121). Her mother and various relatives also tried to make life as agreeable as possible for the rather lonely young girl, and clearly made a special effort at Christmas: in 1832 the Princess noted in her diary that "Mamma gave me a lovely pink bag which she had worked on herself with a little sachet likewise done by her ... and a pink satin dress and a cloak trimmed with fur. Aunt Sophia gave me a dress which she had worked herself."

The young Victoria was also allowed to make the best of Kensington Gardens and Hyde Park, where many contemporaries observed her being driven or, when a little older, riding with surprising freedom. The Princess's most enjoyable times as a young girl, however, seem to have been those spent at her Uncle Leopold's house at Claremont, near Esher (Surrey) – "the brightest epoch of my otherwise rather melancholy childhood". In the years leading up to her accession, life at Kensington was also overshadowed by the presence and activities of Sir John Conroy, a former friend and equerry of her father's but now the Duchess's Chamberlain and confidant. Exerting great influence over the Duchess, he did all he could to ensure that this would continue once Victoria was queen or, better still, during the Duchess's regency – a likely prospect if the aged King William IV died before his niece was eighteen years old. In order to maintain the Princess's supposed dependence on her mother, and so on him, he instituted "regulations" to deprive her of external contacts; her half-brother later called this regime the "Kensington system". Victoria, not surprisingly, detested Conroy and refused the demands for a peerage, a pension and a position at court that he made at her accession.

One person the Princess did meet at Kensington, however – for the first time, and with momentous consequences – was her cousin Prince Albert. It was an encounter arranged by the Duchess and King Leopold with the possibility of an eventual marriage very much in mind. Albert arrived at the palace with his father and his brother, Ernest, on 18 May 1836 and stayed for nearly a month. On the first day the sixteen-year-old Princess entertained the three of them in her sitting-room, and in the evening wrote in her journal that she found Albert "extremely handsome ... c'est à la fois [at the same time] full of goodness and sweetness and very clever and intelligent". It was an auspicious beginning. A few days later the Duchess held what Victoria described as a "great dinner", and on the 30th a "grand ball". On this occasion both the Duchess's own rooms and large parts of the State Apartments, approached through the Stone Gallery and up the King's Stair, were pressed into service, specially decorated and filled with the music of several bands and orchestras; by all

RIGHT 119. *Princess Victoria aged four, by Stephen Poyntz Denning, 1823. As Victoria later wrote, she was then "very much indulged by everyone", and by all accounts already showed the determination and flashes of the 'Hanoverian' bad temper that she occasionally displayed as an adult.*

MIDDLE RIGHT 120. *Princess Victoria's dolls' house, which remained at Kensington after her departure in 1837 and was remarked upon by numerous visitors later in the century. Since 1898 the dolls' house and other toys have been on display to the public in or near the rooms she lived in as a child.*

BOTTOM RIGHT 121. *A selection from among the survivors of the 132 dolls dressed at Kensington by Princess Victoria and her governess, Louise Lehzen, in the early 1830s. The designs of the dresses were based on those worn by fashionable visitors or illustrated in women's journals, and each doll was named after a society figure. From 1898 onwards these, or others like them, were to be favourite exhibits at the palace.*

RIGHT 122. *Louise Lehzen,*
drawn by Princess Victoria in
1833. Sitting to the right is the
Princess's beloved spaniel, Dash,
for whom she also made suits of
clothes, including a "scarlet coat
and blue trousers".

BELOW 123. *Princess Victoria*
riding in a pony carriage in
Kensington Gardens, showing
the East Front of the palace in
the background. The Princess
seems to have been allowed
remarkable freedom to ride
and drive about the gardens,
although always in the company
of one or more grooms. Drawn
and engraved by John Doyle
and published in 1829.

engaged James Wyatt's nephew, Jeffry, who had found favour through his work at Windsor Castle for George IV and in 1824, with the King's permission, changed his name to Wyatville.

In their fullest form, as put forward in 1832, Wyatville's proposals included the construction of a single-storey kitchen block to the north of the north-east pavilion (fig. 124) and, with the King's permission, the taking in of a specified number of the King's state rooms, with the proviso that "in appropriating these Apartments it would be proper to retain their present arrangement and character, in the event of future use". In the event, although the kitchen block was abandoned, by 1835 a substantial programme had been completed, which included the flooring-over of the chapel (until then still occupying the height of two floors beneath the Presence Chamber) and the conversion of a former kitchen at the far western side of the palace to replace it (fig. 126). In addition, the King's State Bedchamber was refitted as a bedroom for the Duchess and the Princess (fig. 127), several adjoining rooms were adapted for their use and the King's Gallery was divided, without the King's knowledge or consent, into three, the easternmost room being the Princess's sitting-room. However disastrous the impact of this last operation on the finest room in the palace, Victoria was delighted, writing in 1836 that "our new sleeping and sitting apartments ... are very lofty and handsome ... our bedroom is very large and lofty and is very nicely furnished ... the old gallery is partitioned into 3 large, lofty fine and cheerful rooms ... one of these ... is my sitting room, and is <u>very</u> prettily furnished".

King William, however, was less impressed. On 20 August 1836 he went to Kensington, according to Charles Greville, "to look about it", his suspicion aroused by a recent quarrel with the Duchess on another issue, and found that she had "appropriated for her own use a suite of apartments, seventeen in number". On getting back to Windsor that evening he told the Duchess "loudly, publicly, and in a tone of displeasure", that

a most unwarrantable liberty had been taken with one of his Palaces; that he had just come from Kensington, where He found apartments had been taken possession of not only without his consent, but contrary to his commands, and that he neither understood nor would endure conduct so disrespectful to him.

It was on the next day, his birthday, that King William made a brutal speech in which he expressed the hope that he would live long enough for Victoria to succeed as queen, and not be placed under a regency led by the Duchess. The wish was granted: he died on 20 June 1837, exactly a month after the Princess's eighteenth birthday.

accounts it must have been the most splendid occasion to have taken place at Kensington since the time of George II. The festivities were presided over by a bust of the Duke of Kent, rather in the manner of Prince Albert's posthumous appearances in the later life of the widowed Queen.

Meanwhile, at the Duchess's instigation, some major alterations had been made to the palace itself. When George IV died in 1830 and the Princess had become heir presumptive, her mother, encouraged by Leopold and influenced by the supposed unhealthiness of their relatively dark and low-ceilinged rooms, had swiftly demanded rather grander accommodation. In 1832, writing to the Prime Minister, Lord Grey, she suggested that "the State Apartment here, which is unoccupied, or used for old pictures, may afford at a small expense the accommodation the Princess and myself require". To show how this might be done she

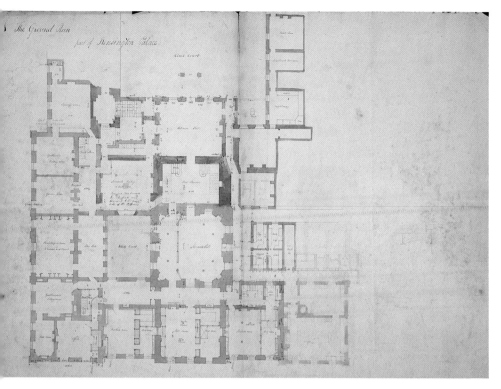

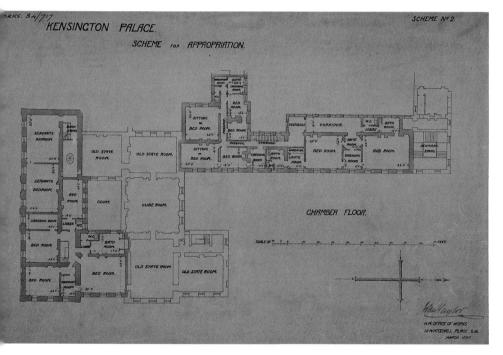

KENSINGTON PALACE.

SCHEME FOR APPROPRIATION.

SCHEME Nº 2

CHAMBER FLOOR.

TOP 124. *Plan of 1832 by Sir Jeffry Wyatville, showing proposals for alterations to the ground or basement floor of the palace for the Duchess of Kent. The block sketched in to the north-east (lower right), intended to contain a kitchen, was not built.*

ABOVE 125. *Plan at State Apartment level, showing the partitions inserted into the former King's Gallery for the Duchess of Kent and her daughter in 1835. The plan was prepared in 1897 to show part of the accommodation then being proposed for Princess Beatrice, Queen Victoria's youngest daughter (below).*

The Duke of Sussex

Following the arrival of the Duke of Kent at Kensington, his brother Augustus Frederick, Duke of Sussex, was also granted apartments there. As his *Times* obituarist put it, "Of all the sons of George III, the Duke of Sussex was, after the Duke of York the most popular; and next his eldest brother, the most accomplished." Victoria apart, he stands out as one of the palace's most interesting nineteenth-century residents.

Between the ages of seventeen and thirty-three the Prince spent most of his time abroad, partly as a result of his long affair with and brief marriage to Lady Augusta Murray (illegal under the Royal Marriages Act of 1772) and partly to alleviate his asthma. In 1806, however, the affair ended and his health improved; he returned to England, was created Duke of Sussex, and was given an enhanced income and apartments at Kensington Palace. The initial plan, as an Office of Works official explained to John Yenn, was that he should occupy the "house formerly in the possession of Mrs Middleton", the recently deceased Under-Housekeeper. However, the house in question – almost certainly the head Housekeeper's lodging that Mrs Middleton had temporarily occupied – was found to be in a poor state, and the Duke himself proposed another arrangement, taking in a substantial part of the Stone Gallery range.

Although the Duke was without pretensions to real scholarship himself, his abiding interest was in his books, which by 1827 already numbered 50,000 and formed one of the most important English private libraries ever assembled. By 1820, when described by Thomas Faulkner in his *History and Antiquities of Kensington*, it was housed in six rooms, one of them being the wide first-floor corridor over the Stone Gallery (fig. 131) and grouped under the headings of Law, Divinity, "Dictionaries, Grammars in all languages and periodical works", history, Greek and Latin classics, and biography. At that stage, Faulkner tells us, it was the Duke's intention "to open this library for the benefit of the public as soon as the whole shall be properly arranged", a process in the hands of his librarian, T.J. Pettigrew, who published a catalogue, with facsimile illustrations by George Cruikshank. As the library grew, so did the need for space, and it seems that in about 1810 George III permitted him to extend his apartments further into the Stone Gallery range, forcing the reluctant departure of a number of long-standing residents, although still, apparently, leaving the gallery itself as an unobstructed route to the King's Stair.

In 1831 the Duke married Lady Cecilia Buggin, widowed daughter of the Earl of Arran. This marriage was as illegal as his first, but in 1840 Queen Victoria was persuaded to create Cecilia Duchess of Inverness in her own right – corresponding to one of the Duke's

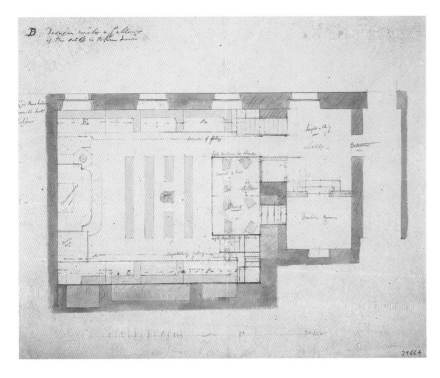

own titles. In his later years the Duke achieved great popularity and at his death, in 1843, his lying in state at Kensington was attended by up to 20,000 people, who filed into the palace and out again via a wooden staircase from a first-floor window (figs. 130, 132). His widow lived on at Kensington until 1873, after which her apartments were occupied by Queen Victoria's fourth daughter, Princess Louise.

The accession of Queen Victoria

Two of the most celebrated events in Kensington's history took place on 20 June 1837: the arrival of the news that Victoria was Queen, and her first Privy Council meeting. On that day, after a month's illness, William IV died early in the morning at Windsor, and the Lord Chamberlain and the Archbishop of Canterbury made straight for Kensington. As the Princess herself described it:

> I was awoke at 6 o'clock by Mamma who told me that the archbishop of Canterbury and Lord Conyngham were here and wished to see me. I got out of bed and went into my sitting room (only in my dressing gown) and alone, and saw them. Lord Conyngham then acquainted me that my poor Uncle, the King, was no more ... and consequently that I am Queen.

Three hours later she received the Prime Minister, Lord Melbourne, made plain her long-considered intention to keep him in office, and at 11.00 am attended her first meeting of the Privy Council in what is now called the Red Saloon (fig. 134).

TOP 126. *One of a series of proposals by Jeffry Wyatville for the creation of a new chapel within a former kitchen on the west side of the Prince of Wales's Court, more or less as carried out in 1833. The blocked fireplaces can be seen within the thickness of the walls at the bottom and to the right. North is to the right, and the windows at the top overlook Palace Green.*

ABOVE 127. *Princess Victoria's Bedroom. It was here that the young Princess was awoken in the early hours of 20 June 1837 with the news of the death of her uncle, William IV, and of her accession to the throne. The room owes much of its appearance today to Queen Mary, who had this and the adjoining rooms redecorated and furnished in the 1930s to evoke their appearance when occupied by the Princess and her mother (fig. 167).*

RIGHT 128. *The chapel as restored for Her Majesty The Queen's Golden Jubilee in 2002.*

BELOW LEFT 129. *Augustus Frederick, Duke of Sussex, by Guy Head, 1798. The fourth son of George III, the Duke lived at Kensington from 1806 until 1843.*

BOTTOM LEFT 130. *The room in which the Duke of Sussex died, as depicted in the* Pictorial Times *in 1843 – a rare view of a royal resident's apartment from before the mid-nineteenth century. The room was probably on the first floor of the Stone Gallery range, looking southwards over Kensington Gardens.*

BELOW RIGHT 131. *Part of the Duke of Sussex's library, housed in the first-floor corridor running the length of the south range to Clock Court, above William III's Stone Gallery. The drawing is by George Cruikshank, who also illustrated the published catalogue of the Duke's books and knew the library well.*

BOTTOM RIGHT 132. *Visitors to the lying in state of the Duke of Sussex in 1843 leaving the palace by a temporary staircase, descending from a window in the King's Gallery range.*

95

Although, as Charles Greville, now Clerk to the Privy Council, recorded in his diary, "her extreme youth and inexperience, and the ignorance of the world concerning her, naturally excited intense curiosity", worries that the task ahead would prove too much for her were quickly dispelled. Greville continued: "She bowed to the Lords, took her seat, and then read her speech in a clear, distinct and audible voice, and without any appearance of fear or embarrassment ... going through the whole ceremony ... with perfect calmness and self possession, but at the same time with a graceful modesty and propriety particularly interesting and ingratiating." The Duke of Wellington, deeply impressed, wrote that "she was as gracious in her manner as if she had been performing the part for years", and others present have left similar impressions.

In the last years of William IV's reign there had been some speculation that the Queen might remain at Kensington and re-establish it as the sovereign's second London home, partly because Nash's massive additions to Buckingham Palace, begun for George IV, were still incomplete. Nevertheless, Victoria herself was in no doubt that she would move there,

133. *Queen Victoria receiving the news of her accession at Kensington Palace, early in the morning of 20 June 1837, as imagined in 1880 by Henry Tanworth Wells. Kneeling to the right is the Archbishop of Canterbury, William Howley, and to the left the Lord Chamberlain, Lord Conyngham. When shown the picture the Queen remarked that "Lord Conyngham who is kneeling should not have a grey coat but a black one. His hair was very dark not reddish. The Archbishop should not have a Cloak on but the usual dress of a Bishop."*

134. Queen Victoria's first Privy Council meeting, as depicted by Sir David Wilkie in 1838. It was held at 11.00 am in the Red Saloon on the day of her accession. To make her stand out the artist shows the Queen wearing a white dress, but being in mourning for the King she actually wore a black one. The dress still exists, and was exhibited at Kensington Palace in 2001.

135. Buckingham Palace from St James's Park by N. Whittock, showing the building as it appeared in 1837, on the partial completion of its remodelling by Edward Blore. When the Queen moved in, in July of that year, more building work soon became necessary.

writing to Leopold on 3 July that she hoped to do so straight after the King's funeral. In fact she had little choice, as Kensington, its State Apartments divided up or dilapidated and surrounded by what was, since its opening to the public by William IV, effectively a public park, was in no fit state to function as the sovereign's residence. In addition, the move asserted her independence, particularly of her mother and the ghastly Conroy. It was not made, though, without regret. A few days before her departure she wrote, again to her uncle: "I <u>really</u> and <u>truly</u> go into Buckingham Palace the day after to-morrow, but I must say, though I am very glad to do so, I feel sorry to leave for <u>ever</u> my poor old birthplace." Later in the reign, her nostalgia for Kensington was to have a major impact on its future – even on its survival.

Victorian KENSINGTON 1837–98

The palace becomes the home of Princess Louise, daughter of Queen Victoria, and the Duke and Duchess of Teck whose first child, later Queen Mary, is born there in 1867. Structural decay and schemes for demolition are averted, and the State Apartments are restored and opened to the public in 1898. Kensington Gardens, although now simplified in design, become a place of fashionable recreation.

LEFT 136. *Princess Louise's statue of Queen Victoria in her coronation robes, commissioned by the Kensington Women's Jubilee Fund to commemorate the Queen's Golden Jubilee in 1887, and unveiled in the Queen's presence in 1893. As was common practice at the time, the marble was carved by a professional, working from a clay model prepared by the Princess. Her friend Alfred Gilbert – best known for the Eros statue in Piccadilly – may have had a hand in its design. The photograph was taken in about 1900 and shows, to the right, the greenhouses that were soon to be replaced by the Sunken Garden.*

FAR RIGHT 137. *Colonel Chaine and his wife, Maria (née Phipps), Kensington's State Housekeeper, photographed in 1897 outside their apartment in Clock Court. The holder of an office created in 1837, although with few real duties, Mrs Chaine lived at Kensington with a substantial household from 1867 until 1915.*

RIGHT 138. *Princess Sophia, born in 1777, the thirteenth child of George III and Queen Charlotte. Except for a five-year period when the palace was under repair, she occupied an apartment at Kensington from 1820 until her death in 1848. Miniature by Richard Cosway dated 1792.*

The palace community, 1837–98

The most prominent residents at Kensington Palace during Queen Victoria's reign were her daughter Princess Louise and the Duke and Duchess of Teck, parents of the future Queen Mary, whose apartments and activities at Kensington are described below. They were not, however, the only members of the royal family to live there during this period. In the early years the Duke of Sussex was still alive, and his widow continued to live at Kensington until 1873. The Duke's sister, Princess Sophia, had an apartment there from about 1820 until her death in 1848 – except for the years 1838–43, when the palace's "ruinous condition" forced her to use a house nearby – but thereafter there were no immediate members of the royal family in residence until the arrival of Princess Louise in 1875. Among the non-royal residents were, for example, the succession of individuals and their households who occupied the 'house' on the north side of the Prince of Wales's Court: Lady Caroline Barrington, followed by General Sir Francis

Seymour and, from 1891, by the Dowager Countess Granville (fig. 84), widow of the 2nd Earl Granville, a close adviser of the Queen.

Since the palace's first occupation by William III it had had a chapel and a chaplain, and this remained the case until 1901 when the position was abolished and the chapel closed by the new king, Edward VII (1901–10). From 1834 until 1854 the chaplain was Joseph Jackson and at the end of the period, W.G. Green, both of whom were housed near the chapel on the west side of the Prince of Wales's Court. The larger, private households employed housekeepers at or near the top of their large hierarchies of servants, but in 1837 the Queen saw to the appointment of a Housekeeper of the Private Apartments, with the task of overseeing their smooth running and managing common areas. The first appointee was a Mrs Jordan, who occupied the modest quarters formerly used by the Duchess of Kent's Housekeeper. The historic position of palace Housekeeper, or at least its status and some of its functions, lived on in that of State Housekeeper, a post held from 1837 to 1867 by Lady Augusta Gordon Hallyburton, daughter of the Duke of Clarence and the actress with whom he lived for many years (another Mrs Jordan); her successor was

TOP 139. *The Tecks' saloon, photographed in about 1870. The Duke and Duchess lived at Kensington from 1867 until 1882, and their first daughter, later Queen Mary, was born there soon after they arrived.*

MIDDLE 140. *The Duke and Duchess of Teck with Princess May (on the Duke's knee) in their garden at Kensington, facing the palace's East Front, in 1868.*

BOTTOM 141. *View of the Duke and Duchess's East Front garden in about 1900, looking eastwards over Kensington Gardens. The planting scheme and layout is substantially that praised and recorded in* The Gardener's Magazine *in 1868, where it is attributed to the Duke.*

Maria Chaine (née Phipps), daughter of Prince Albert's Private Secretary, at whose death in 1915 the post was abolished. Alongside them and other residents lived a vast number of servants and private household officials who completed the palace community.

The Duke and Duchess of Teck

The best known among Kensington Palace's royal residents in the second half of the nineteenth century is a young girl, Victoria Mary ('May') of Teck, who was to marry George, Prince of Wales in 1893 and become Queen Mary on his accession in 1910. Victoria Mary's mother was Mary Adelaide, daughter of George III's son Adolphus, Duke of Cambridge – she was amiable, popular, generously built and known as 'Fat Mary'. In 1866 she married Prince Franz of Teck, only son of Duke (later King) Alexander of Württemberg, who, in 1871, was granted the status of Duke of Teck, the title by which he is best known. As the couple had few resources of their own, the Queen granted them the apartments at Kensington that she had once occupied. Used only for storage since the departure of the Duchess and Queen Victoria in 1837, the rooms required a good deal of expensive work and redecoration, in which the Duke took a strong personal interest and for which he had a considerable gift – a talent that his eldest daughter inherited. His interests also extended to the gardens that went with the apartment, immediately to the east of the palace, where the work of this "noble amateur" was praised in *The Gardener's Magazine* of 1868.

Shortly after the Tecks' arrival at Kensington, in July 1867, their first daughter was born in the former King's Bedchamber, which had been largely reconstructed in 1816–19 and had been refitted for the Duchess of Kent and Princess Victoria in 1832–35; the King's Bedchamber was used because the bedroom

142. *Princess Louise, photographed in Venice in about 1890. She lived at Kensington from 1875 until 1939.*

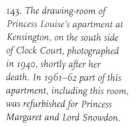

143. *The drawing-room of Princess Louise's apartment at Kensington, on the south side of Clock Court, photographed in 1940, shortly after her death. In 1961–62 part of this apartment, including this room, was refurbished for Princess Margaret and Lord Snowdon.*

the Duchess of Teck was to occupy, on the floor below, was not yet ready. Queen Victoria left an account of her visit to the new baby: "Franz received me at the door, and we went up to the top of the house, where I lived the last two years; and here, in the former bedroom, in which Mama and I slept, I found dear Mary, Aunt Cambridge and the baby – a very fine child."

Much as the Tecks liked Kensington, their dire finances, not helped by having taken on a second home (White Lodge in Richmond Park), forced them to leave for the Continent in 1882. However, just as Queen Victoria's attachment to her birthplace affected its treatment in the later years of her reign, so did Princess May's – as both Princess of Wales and Queen Mary – influence its use during the twentieth century.

Princess Louise

Looking out over Kensington Gardens is a marble statue of Queen Victoria, which she herself unveiled, aged seventy-four, in 1893 (fig. 136). It is a fine memorial to Victoria, but perhaps a better one to its designer, Princess Louise, in many ways the most talented and least conventional of the Queen's five daughters and, from 1875 to 1939, a vital part of the life of the palace (fig. 142).

In 1871, after refusing a long series of foreign princes, Louise married John Campbell, Marquess of Lorne, heir to the 8th Duke of Argyll and head of the Clan Campbell – the first marriage of a sovereign's daughter outside royalty since that of Princess Mary, Henry VIII's sister, in 1515. Their first London home was a rented house, but following the death of the Duke of Sussex's widow in 1873 they were given the use of her apartments (or a large part of them) at Kensington, and moved in in February 1875. Apart from their absence between 1878 and 1883, during the Marquess's term as Governor-General of Canada, this remained their main London home, even after Lorne's succession to the dukedom in 1900. Much of the apartment, largely untouched since the death of the Duke of Sussex in 1843, and not substantially refurbished since the reign of George III, was in poor condition and required a great deal of work – including the dismantling of large numbers of the Duke of Sussex's decaying bookshelves – to make it habitable. When it came to the garden, advice was given by the celebrated gardener Gertrude Jekyll, who may also have helped with the interior. As the Victoria statue shows, however, Princess Louise was herself an artist of professional standard, and it is for this, apart perhaps from charity work, that she is best known. Arguably the most gifted member of a very artistic family, she was also the first to be trained outside the home – although not, as she regretted, enough. After 1868 she attended, so far as her other duties permitted, the National Art Training School in South Kensington

146. *The King's Drawing Room as it appeared at the reopening of the palace to the public in 1899. The intention was at least to evoke the mid-eighteenth-century appearance of the State Apartments and to present the building "as a Palace not a picture gallery".*

house to her youngest daughter, Princess Beatrice, after the death of her husband, Prince Henry of Battenberg, in 1896, and to her third daughter, Princess Helena, married to Prince Christian of Schleswig-Holstein. When Kensington was put forward as the only viable option, it became clear that the necessary work would be extremely expensive and, in order for it to be acceptable to Parliament, the Queen and the Government struck a bargain. According to this, as Reginald Brett (2nd Viscount Esher from 1899), Secretary of the Office of Works, explained to a colleague in 1897, the Queen would make the Ranger's Lodge at Greenwich, Kew Palace and Queen Charlotte's Cottage available for sale, lease or some other use in return for this accommodation being provided. Crucially, Brett also recommended that, in conjunction with preparing apartments for the two princesses, the Orangery and the 'State Rooms' – both in "disgraceful" condition – should also be restored. The latter, he suggested, might induce the Queen "to consent to the appropriation of the State Rooms to some public use in the nature of a museum, or at any rate to opening them to the public at certain periods of the year". Provided that the Queen's permission was forthcoming and that the building work could be complete by April 1898, the Treasury, to Brett's surprise and delight, agreed to provide all the necessary funds. Victoria's formal approval swiftly followed, to the effect that "Her

Majesty desired that the State Rooms of Kensington Palace, which have been unoccupied since October 1760, should be put into proper repair and returned as nearly as possible to their former condition, with a view to their being opened to the Public during her Majesty's Pleasure."

The restoration of 1898

Once the decision had been taken, the first priority was the poor condition of the building, which was riddled with rotten and collapsing floors, leaking roofs and subsiding walls, and which in the case of the Queen's Gallery range (fig. 145) had gone so far that demolition seemed almost unavoidable. Numerous fit-tings inserted earlier in the century, such as the kitchen range in the Queen's Gallery and partition walls (notably those inserted for the Duchess of Kent in the King's Gallery), were swept away, and a new access route for visitors contrived from the Queen's Staircase porch. Central heating was installed in the main rooms, but lighting – possibly for fear of fire – was not. The work was carried out by the long-established private firm of John Mowlem, under the general supervision of Sir John Taylor – since 1867 the Surveyor of Royal Palaces, Public Buildings and Royal Parks for the Ministry of Works (established in 1851 and now in control of the three Commissioners). Site supervision was provided by Mr Philip, temporary Clerk of Works, and the decoration and finishing of the interiors (including the selection and placing of the furniture and pictures) was supervised by Charles Robinson. In this he was assisted by Ernest Law, a knowledgeable if self-promoting lawyer-turned-historian and author of a catalogue of the Hampton Court pictures published in 1881.

The objectives of the work and the thinking behind them were set out by Reginald Brett in a letter to Taylor: "In restoring the palace," he wrote, "it is desirable to adhere strictly to the details of which we have record so that the decoration when complete may appear as far as possible exactly what it was in the reign of George II." In cautioning Taylor he may have had in mind the architect's heedless destruction in the late 1880s of important medieval fabric at the Tower of London – and, no doubt, the loudly voiced philosophy of the Society for the Protection of Ancient Buildings, which had cut its teeth over the same incident. Brett's overall intention – foreshadowing that behind the restoration of Hampton Court Palace after 1986 – was to make it look like a "Palace not a picture gallery", mindful no doubt of the gallery-like appearance of Hampton Court in his own time. In achieving this, as Law's 1898 *Guidebook* to Kensington tells us, careful attention was paid "never to renew any decoration where it was possible to preserve it – least of all ever to attempt to 'improve' old work into new. On the contrary, repairing, patching, mending, piecing, cleaning have been the main occupations of the decorators which would render some impatient, slapdash builders and surveyors frantic." Law was probably right in adding that "never before ... has the restoration of any historic public building been carried out with quite the same

amount of loving care". In fact, their understanding of the building's architectural history and its appearance in 1760, based largely on illustrations in W.H. Pyne's three-volume *History of the Royal Residences* of 1819 (figs. 2, 82, 113) and Thomas Faulkner's *History and Antiquities of Kensington* of 1820, was very poor and led them into numerous errors of detail; it was not until the work of Patrick Faulkner and George Chettle in the 1950s, and Howard Colvin and John Newman in the 1970s, that a real understanding was developed. Nevertheless, the philosophy and intent behind the restoration of Kensington in 1898, whatever its short-comings, made it something of a landmark in the conservation of historic buildings and their presentation to the public.

When it came to decorating and furnishing the interiors, an emphasis was laid on stripping down the panelling to bare wood, covering the walls with paper printed in patterns based on eighteenth-century damask, and cleaning and touching up the original gilding and painting. Among the more spectacular successes were the King's Staircase paintings, found in a state from which "it seemed impossible" that they could be rescued, and the King's Gallery, restored, if not precisely to its eighteenth-century appearance, at least to its full volume. Exceptions to the eighteenth-century theme, however, were the bedroom – once William III's Great Bedchamber – and the dressing room that had been used by the Duchess of Kent and the young Victoria, which, although dilapidated, remained much as they had left them and were restored in their honour. Of the pictures, selected (with some exceptions) on the basis that they related to the period during which Kensington Palace was inhabited as a royal residence, 157 came from Hampton Court, while others were borrowed from the National Portrait Gallery. A request for further items from Windsor Castle or Buckingham Palace was, for the moment, refused, on the grounds that their selection and hang had been determined by the late Prince Consort and were not to be disturbed.

In January 1898, while work was still in progress, the palace was opened to the press, which greeted it with great enthusiasm, *The Times* seeing in the project a chance "To endow London with another Hampton Court". They were reminded, however, that "Kensington remained a Royal Palace to be occupied at any time by the Sovereign ... not a public building handed over for the perpetual enjoyment of the public." Following a brief preview by the Queen, the public opening followed on 24 May 1899 and was an instant success, attracting over 340,000 visitors in the first twelve months – more than in any single year in the following century. From then until 1913 the State Apartments and the newly restored Orangery were open every day of the year, except Wednesdays, Christmas Day and Good Friday, until six o'clock in

147. *Queen Victoria's visit to Kensington, on 15 May 1899, to inspect the newly refurbished State Apartments, due to be opened to the public later in the month. Her Private Secretary and guide, Lord Stamfordham, described taking the Queen around her old home as a "most interesting and in many ways moving experience".*

ABOVE 148. *Early visitors to Kensington Palace admiring Princess Victoria's dolls' house and other toys, under the eye of a smart frock-coated warder.*

TOP RIGHT 149. *Two ladies, probably nursery maids or nannies, pushing prams along Dial Walk in Kensington Gardens in about 1890. This was a common sight from the 1870s until recent times.*

MIDDLE RIGHT 150. *Launching a model schooner on the Round Pond, as depicted in* The Graphic *of 15 August 1874, with the palace in the background. The action appears to be interesting at least three generations of the family, while to the left a uniformed page waits holding a model cutter.*

BOTTOM RIGHT 151. *Illustration by Arthur Rackham for J.M. Barrie's* Peter Pan in Kensington Gardens *of 1906, showing children playing in the snow-covered avenue to the west side of the south gardens. Barrie's works have planted Kensington Gardens firmly in the minds of generations of children, and since 1912 Peter Pan himself has been represented by a statue on the south side of the Serpentine.*

the summer, but – in the absence of artificial light – until four o'clock in winter. The apartments and their visitors were in the hands of five warders during the daytime, while professional supervision of the contents was provided by the Caretaker of the Pictures at Hampton Court, Mr J. Brown, and security by two policemen on night duty.

Kensington Gardens, 1837–98

During Queen Victoria's reign the long process of simplification that had begun to affect Kensington Gardens in the 1760s continued. By the 1840s, although the basic geometry of Bridgeman's layout remained intact (fig. 154), and much of his planting survived, the more detailed and labour-intensive parts had been radically altered. The 'serpentine' paths so carefully laid out through the blocks of planting around the Great Bow (fig. 104) had disappeared, while the gardens between the Serpentine and the eastern boundary had been replaced by trees and grass. Probably from the end of the eighteenth century, but certainly by the early 1820s, the western two-thirds of the Wilderness had been put down to pasture and the geometry of the eastern part largely destroyed, although Wise's Sunken Garden survived for a few more years as an earthwork; after 1845 the western-most sector was surrendered for the creation of a new road, Kensington Palace Gardens (see below). By the middle of the century the blocks of planting between the principal rides in the main gardens to the east of the palace, increasingly informal in appearance, were traversed by paths with no relation to the eighteenth-century plan.

Although the administrative difference between Kensington Gardens and Hyde Park remained, and horses and carriages were still excluded, the physical boundary between them became gradually less apparent: the 'bastioned' wall and ditch dividing

Kensington Gardens and Hyde Park was destroyed at various stages from 1833 onwards, and in the late 1830s, at the Queen's request, the wall behind it was replaced with railings. Substantial changes were made to the immediate surroundings of the palace gardens, including the Duke of Teck's garden, laid out to his own designs after 1867 (fig. 141). By the 1890s the area between the Orangery and the palace and to the south-east was taken up by sheds and cold frames, and remained so until the essentials of the present

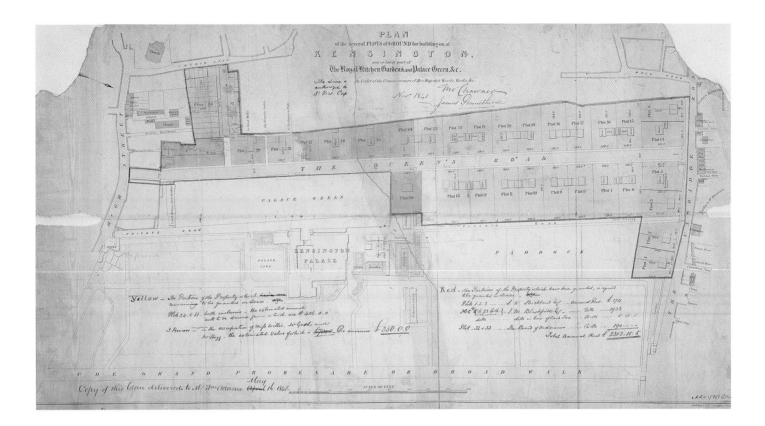

ABOVE 152. *Plan of the surroundings of the palace to the west and north-west prepared in 1841, setting out proposals for the development of Kensington Palace Gardens, covering a large part of the old Palace Green and the western half of the Wilderness. The "forcing ground" was set aside for the new barracks, which were eventually completed in 1858 and replaced by the existing buildings in 1905. North is to the right.*

RIGHT 153. *The Crystal Palace, put up on the south side of Hyde Park to house the Great Exhibition of 1851, one of the spectacular success stories of Victorian England. View by William Wyld, 1851.*

planting were laid out, along with the new Sunken Garden, in 1908 (fig. 155).

The gardens had been open to everyone, without charge, since the previous reign; now their use and popularity increased rapidly as land to the north and south of Kensington Gardens and Hyde Park became built up. From mid-century onwards the gardens took on one of their most enduringly familiar functions – a promenade for pram-pushing nannies and nursery maids (fig. 149) – while by the 1870s the Round Pond

was already a celebrated meeting place for model-boat enthusiasts, young and old (fig. 150). As public use increased, so facilities for visitors were provided and improved, including the first Refreshment Room in 1855, numerous drinking fountains and, in 1899, the first public lavatories.

The biggest single change to the immediate environs of the palace in Queen Victoria's reign, however, took place to the west of the buildings. In 1840 a Treasury Committee, set up two years earlier to investigate the

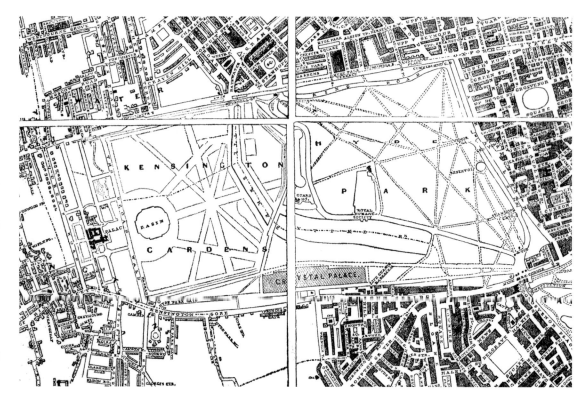

154. *Detail of James Wyld's 'New Plan of London', published in 1851 to accompany the Great Exhibition. Although to the east of the palace the bones of Bridgeman's layout are still apparent, the Wilderness has largely disappeared, partly replaced by Kensington Palace Gardens, which had then been under construction for about five years. Note also the extent to which the surroundings of Kensington Gardens and Hyde Park had by then become built up (compare with fig. 104), and the size and position of the Crystal Palace itself.*

155. *The Sunken Garden, installed immediately to the west of the palace in 1908–09. For the previous thirty years or so the site had been occupied by cold frames and greenhouses, used for bringing on bedding plants for use elsewhere in the gardens (fig. 136).*

management of the royal gardens, decided that the kitchen gardens or "forcing ground" at Kensington, which since the seventeenth century had occupied a site to the west of the south end of Palace Green (figs. 107, 152), should be given up. Once it had been allowed by a special Act of Parliament of 1841 "to grant building leases of the Royal Gardens at Kensington and to form and improve other Royal Gardens", plans were made to sell it off, together with a strip of similar width running north to the Bayswater Road, and to create what became Kensington Palace Gardens. In spite of opposition led by the architect J.C. Loudon, and his urgings in *The Times* that Hyde Park, Kensington Gardens and the park of Holland House should be linked together in one unbroken landscape,

in 1843 James Pennethorne was commissioned to survey the site and lay out the new development. Between 1845 and 1868 a series of about twenty-five villas in a range of Italianate styles was put up, designed by architects including Sir Charles Barry, Decimus Burton and Sidney Smirke. The result was, and remains, one of the most remarkable streets in London but, in addition to obstructing Loudon's scheme, it entailed a few architectural casualties, including the former Foot Guards' barracks put up in the 1690s to the west of the palace (fig. 33), still in use until 1845, and by 1850 Vanbrugh's water tower of 1719 (fig. 85).

156. Bronze statue of William III by the German sculptor Heinrich Baucke, presented to Edward VII in 1907 by the King's nephew Kaiser Wilhelm II and installed on the South Front of the palace.

CROWN FRAME OF GEORGE I, 1715
Coronation crown of George I. Crown cap a later replacement. Crown frame of gold, silver and gilt. Cat. no.3

The PALACE *in the* TWENTIETH CENTURY

The newly formed London Museum finds a temporary home in the State Apartments on the eve of the First World War. Queen Victoria's youngest daughter, Beatrice, lives on at the palace until 1940, and a new generation of royal residents, among them Princess Margaret, moves in during the following decades. Bomb damage is slowly repaired, and improvements are made to the display of the State Apartments. The London Museum returns in 1951 and remains until 1975.

LEFT 157. *A series of crown frames, exhibited as part of a display of coronation costume at the London Museum, Kensington Palace, in 1973. Many of these are now on permanent display at the Tower of London.*

The London Museum, 1911–13

The eve of the First World War saw a strange interlude in the history of the royal palace, when, between 1911 and 1913, the State Apartments became the first home of the London Museum. Both the origins of the museum and its temporary installation at Kensington partly were due, once again, to Reginald Brett, now Lord Esher, in spite of the fact that such a use of the State Apartments ran quite contrary to the aims of the 1898 restoration. The initial idea for the museum was that of Esher's friend and colleague Lewis Harcourt, son of the Liberal politician Sir William Harcourt, First Commissioner for Works from 1905 to 1910, and friend of the royal family. He had long felt that London deserved something on the lines of the Parisian Musée Carnavalet, installed in a sixteenth-century *hôtel particulier* in the Marais in 1881, which told the story of the city from the remotest times to the early 1800s. Armed with a substantial private benefaction, tremendous confidence and Esher's support, by 1910 Lewis Harcourt was already buying exhibits and investigating possible locations. That Kensington became a possibility was due essentially to the project's appeal, as presented by Harcourt, to Queen Alexandra and Queen Mary, and it was the latter who in 1911 persuaded her husband, the new King George V (1910–36), to offer the State Apartments at Kensington Palace as the temporary home of the 'projected' museum. Esher and Harcourt were immediately appointed as trustees, and the greatly gifted Guy Laking, an expert on arms, armour, Sèvres and a protégé of the late King, was appointed as Keeper.

Through gifts, purchases and finds from City building sites, where deep-basemented buildings were already destroying its buried past, the museum's collection expanded at great speed. Over

RIGHT 158. *The royal party that visited the London Museum on 21 March 1912, here shown inspecting exhibits in the Cupola Room. The King (left) is depicted listening to Lewis Harcourt; to the extreme right is the Keeper, Guy Laking, standing beside Queen Mary, Princess Mary and Prince George (later Duke of Kent). According to* The Times, *George V was in a "merry mood" and thoroughly enjoyed the visit.*

159. *The Presence Chamber in 1912 containing the Coronation Robes of Edward VII and Queen Alexandra. Thanks to the establishment of the Royal Ceremonial Dress Collection at Kensington later in the century, these items are once again kept at the palace and were most recently shown in the exhibition* Coronation Robes: Three Centuries of Royal Splendour *in 1994.*

160. *One of the museum's most celebrated exhibits, the remains of a Roman boat, found during the construction of London's new County Hall and exhibited in a purpose-built annexe at Kensington from 1911 to 1913. At the far end can be seen another prized exhibit: a cell door and various other grim-looking pieces of equipment from Newgate Gaol.*

161. *Princess Beatrice, youngest daughter of Queen Victoria, who lived at Kensington as a widow from 1901 to 1940. Portrait painted in 1908 by Joaquín Sorolla y Bastida.*

rooms she had were essentially those occupied by the Tecks, in addition to some of the lower rooms in the Queen's Gallery range; the early suggestion that she should have use of the carved-up King's Gallery (fig. 125) and the state rooms in the south-east pavilion was overtaken by their restoration and opening to the public in 1898. Before the First World War, Beatrice lived in considerable style, holding a lavish coming-out ball at Kensington in 1905 for her daughter Eugenie ('Ena') who married Alfonso XIII of Spain in the following year. Princess Beatrice remained at Kensington between the wars, engaged among other things in sorting and transcribing her mother's papers, a valiant effort marred only by her deliberate destruction or distortion of so much of the material. An occasional visitor was her great-great-nephew Philip, Prince of Greece and Denmark (now His Royal Highness The Duke of Edinburgh) who stayed at Kensington with his grandmother, the Dowager Marchioness of Milford Haven (daughter of Queen Victoria's daughter Alice and mother of Lord Mountbatten of Burma: see inside back cover) who lived at Kensington between 1922 and 1950. In 1940 Princess Beatrice moved to the country, having been the last royal resident in what was then to become the exclusively 'public' side of the palace. From 1956 until 1960 her son, the Marquess of Carisbrooke, also lived at Kensington on the south side of Clock Court. Princess Alice, Countess of Athlone, daughter of Queen Victoria's son Leopold, lived at the palace from 1922 to 1981, apart from during the war and the several years it took to repair bomb damage to her apartment. Between 1954 and 1968 Kensington was the London home of Princess Marina of Greece, widow of George V's fourth son, the Duke of Kent, and was used as a base from which she carried out her many official engagements (fig. 165). In 1960 the palace community was joined by Princess Margaret and Lord Snowdon, at first living on the north side of the palace but later in the apartment lately occupied by the Marquess of Carisbrooke and in the past successively by the Duke of Sussex, the Duchess of Inverness and Princess Louise. The fine house on the north side of the Prince of Wales's Court, originally fitted out for Frederick, Prince of Wales in 1727 (fig. 84), was occupied from 1891 to 1938 by the Dowager Countess Granville, and then by Lady Patricia Ramsay, daughter of Queen Victoria's third son, Arthur, Duke of Connaught.

the next year the whole of the State Apartments was filled with cases, and the exhibits, grouped roughly according to period, were installed and labelled. The aim was to illustrate and inspire an interest in London and its past, but many exhibits were either of costume, related to the royal family, or both – an anomaly commented on by professionals but much enjoyed by the public. In addition, an annexe was built in the garden just north of the palace to house the remains of a late third-century Roman boat unearthed during the building of County Hall in 1910 (fig. 160). Following a royal preview in March 1912 (fig. 158), the first day of public opening saw an incredible 13,000 visitors admitted, following a crowded route from the foot of the Queen's Staircase and back again, armed with copies of a new edition of Law's guidebook. The London Museum's first spell at Kensington, however, was to be a short one, for in 1912 a more permanent home became available in the form of Lancaster House in St James's, through the generosity of Sir William Lever who bought the lease in that year. Under the terms of a deal struck between him, Lewis Harcourt and the Government, the entire collection was installed there in the early autumn of the following year.

Royal residents and others, 1901–75

Princess Beatrice, Queen Victoria's youngest daughter, whose need for a London home had eventually led to the opening of the State Apartments, finally moved into Kensington with the blessing of her eldest brother, the new King Edward VII, in 1901. The

Alongside the grander residents there were many others, who all had indoor and stable servants, although these rapidly decreased throughout the period as custom changed and cars replaced the horse and carriage. In addition, a number of apartments continued to be given to current and former officials of the Royal Household, granted and occupied (as were those of other non-royal residents) free of rent

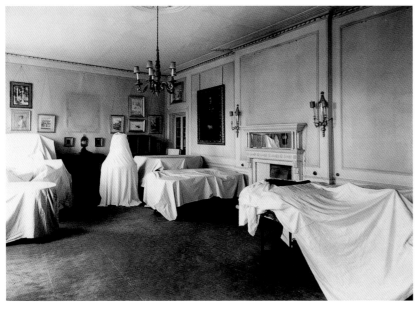

dispatch of more than 5,000 parcels to servicemen and prisoners from their offices in the Queen's Apartments.

In the immediate post-war years, with public interest and governmental energies diverted to other matters, the State Apartments remained closed; that they were opened again in 1923 was thanks to the demands of the Mayor of Kensington, Sir William Davison, and the insistence of Lord Crawford, first Commissioner of Works. Opening was restricted, however, to Saturday afternoons, and visitors were now charged sixpence; after 1926 the apartments were open on Sundays too and, from the mid-1930s until 1939, every day of the week from March to September. Various changes and improvements were carried out in the years that followed, including a major restoration of the King's Staircase paintings, partly to remove the varnish misguidedly applied in 1898. The work carried out between 1933 and 1937, by staff of the Ancient Monuments Section of the Ministry of Works, involved remounting the canvases on wooden panels and patching and retouching areas of the surface. Other improvements included the redecoration of the King's Gallery and the restoration, at the request of Queen Mary, of the Grinling Gibbons carvings in the Presence Chamber, then still covered in layers of paint. The most important presentational change, once again on the Queen's initiative, was to the dressing room and bedroom once used by the Duchess of Kent and Princess Victoria and in which Queen Mary herself had been born. Her intention was that these rooms should be decorated and furnished – as had been half-heartedly attempted in 1898 – to evoke their appearance in the mid-1830s. To this effect the Queen had them redecorated and furnished with appropriate material, much of it genuinely relating to Victoria's life, and the rooms were reopened to a fanfare of publicity in 1936 (figs. 127, 167). The Council Chamber, to the other side of the King's Drawing Room, was filled with further displays, including Victoria's dolls' house and additional material assembled by the Queen.

but otherwise at their own expense, by the 'Grace and Favour' of the sovereign.

The State Apartments, 1913–75

Between the wars
At the outbreak of war in August 1914 the State Apartments at Kensington had already been closed since February 1913, for fear of damage by militant suffragettes who had been calling attention to their cause by renewed attacks on public property. Ten of the Kensington warders were sent to Hampton Court Palace, whose state rooms had reopened in September 1913, while three patrolled the grounds of Kensington Palace. During the war, George V made parts of the palace available for war-work and charitable purposes, and occupants included the Sailors' and Soldiers' Christmas Fund and the Irish Women's Association, which managed a weekly

New uncertainties and a new direction, 1939–75
Although briefly closed on the outbreak of war in 1939, the State Apartments reopened in 1940, closing only in 1944. By then, together with much of the rest of the palace, they were once again in poor condition: bombs had gutted the Queen's Drawing Room and done more extensive damage elsewhere (fig. 168), particularly to the north side of the palace, while military occupation and lack of maintenance of certain areas had taken their toll. The external appearance of the palace, of Kensington Gardens and Hyde Park, stripped of its railings, was a mess, and as an official put it in 1946, if left for much longer "with no heating, no ventilation, dry-rot, and probably

RIGHT 164. *His Royal Highness Prince Philip, Duke of Edinburgh, and his best man, the Marquess of Milford Haven, leaving Kensington Palace on the day of his wedding to Princess Elizabeth on 20 November 1947.*

BELOW LEFT 165. *Princess Marina (centre) and others standing outside the palace during the fire that broke out on 10 January 1963, and which delayed the completion of Princess Margaret and Lord Snowdon's new apartment. Princess Marina, daughter of Prince Nicholas of Greece, married George V's fourth son, George, Duke of Kent, in 1934. She had an apartment at Kensington from 1954 until 1968.*

BELOW RIGHT 166. *Princess Margaret, Lord Snowdon and their children in Clock Court, photographed by Cecil Beaton in 1965.*

167. *The Duchess of Kent's Dressing Room today, substantially as redecorated and furnished in 1936 on Queen Mary's initiative to evoke its appearance exactly a century earlier.*

168. *Damage to the north range of Clock Court and adjoining parts of the Queen's Apartments caused by incendiary bombs in 1940. Shortages of money and materials after the war meant that repairs to some areas had to wait for over thirty years.*

169. Work under way on the restoration of the ceiling paintings in the King's Gallery in 1956, under the leadership of Alastair Stewart, Chief Restorer to the Ministry of Works.

wood-boring beetle, not to mention the exposure of the fabric following bombing, the whole place will rapidly deteriorate". It was a low moment in the palace's history and, given the fate of so many historic buildings at this period, a dangerous one. With regard to the State Apartments and the rooms below them, there were two main problems – what to do with them and, in a period of extreme financial austerity and ferocious controls on building, how to pay for it. Shortly after the death of Princess Beatrice in 1944 it

seems that her apartments were still being considered for residential use, but by 1945 it was felt that "consideration should be given to admitting the public when suitable furnishings or exhibits could be provided". By 1947 plans for the future functions of various parts of the palace had been worked out, although they failed, perhaps, to take advantage of various opportunities: in particular George Chettle, armed with a solid grasp of the building's history, noted that the plans "are still open to the grave objection that they obstruct the

172. *A Georgian shopfront from 181 High Holborn, acquired by the London Museum in about 1913 and first displayed at Lancaster House, shown here in 1952 shortly after the reopening of the museum at Kensington Palace.*

The Queen's pictures, Anthony Blunt, the paintings were rearranged, the King's Gallery was redecorated, the ceiling canvases were restored and a range of royal costumes put on display. The State Apartments reopened in 1956 (figs. 169, 170).

The London Museum returns, 1951–75

The London Museum's enjoyment of Lancaster House, interrupted by the First World War, was brought to an end by the Second World War, and the museum was once again left looking for a new home. As early as 1945 a return to Kensington was being discussed, and in the following year a Government spokesman announced George VI's willingness to allow parts of the palace to be used for this purpose. Nothing was decided immediately and other sites were considered, including, interestingly, the bombed-out shell of Holland House. In 1948, however, the King's offer was accepted, and the museum reopened in the palace in 1951. The space offered at this stage excluded the State Apartments – the museum's previous home – but took up most of the two floors below, largely vacant since Princess Beatrice's departure in 1940; the external doorway she had made to the Red Saloon now became the museum's main entrance. As in 1911, the arrangement was seen as temporary, not least as the palace's layout compromised the chronological order of the displays, and there was far less space even than at Lancaster House. For the palace, however, it was a good move, restoring a real function to the empty floors under the State Apartments and ensuring the repair, servicing and maintenance of the building as a whole.

While at Kensington, the museum successfully expanded its collection and activities, providing services for 1200 school parties a year by 1965, playing an active part once again in the practice and direction of London's archaeology, and, by 1970, attracting over 290,000 visitors a year. At the same time, in addition to its permanent displays, the museum ran a lively programme of temporary exhibitions, usually mounted in a room on the lower-ground floor. The first, *The London of Dickens*, was held in 1954; other themes included *The London of Queen Elizabeth I* held in 1958 (the 400th anniversary of her accession) and, in 1968, a display created by Philippa Glanville entitled *Nonsuch: A Lost Tudor Palace*, the site of which had been recently excavated.

In 1960, however, after a decade of deliberation, plans were laid for the museum's amalgamation with the Guildhall Museum and removal to purpose-built premises in the City. The new institution came into existence, at least on paper, by the Museum of London Act of 1965. Ten years later the galleries at Kensington were closed, and in December 1976 the Museum of London opened in its new buildings at London Wall.

architecturally and historically logical approach to the King's staircase, leaving it as a foolish cul-de-sac only to be viewed from its top landing during the tour (in reverse of the planned order) of the state rooms". In the event the approach he was referring to, via the Stone Gallery, remained blocked, as it had been since the second half of the nineteenth century, but many practical improvements were made, including, at last, the installation of electric light. In June 1949 the State Apartments were reopened to the public, followed two years later by the rooms below, in the hands of the London Museum. Although the State Apartments were once again displayed as a "Palace not a gallery", as Law and Esher had intended, their appearance was not really satisfactory. In 1953, however, the suggestion by Her Majesty The Queen that the museum should contain a room dedicated to Queen Mary, which could not have been accommodated in the existing space, led in 1955 to the takeover of the State Apartments by the museum. In collaboration with the Surveyor of

KENSINGTON
since the 1970s

New royal residents include the Prince and Princess of Wales; the Princess's death leads to extraordinary scenes of public mourning. Further improvements are made to the display of the State Apartments, the Royal Ceremonial Dress Collection is installed and a collection of dresses belonging to Diana, Princess of Wales is put on display.

LEFT 173. *The 'Clock of the Four Great Monarchies', made by Charles Clay, Clockmaker to the Board of Works, and completed by John Pyke in 1743. It was installed in the Cupola Room during the reign of George III, removed in the early nineteenth century and reinstated there in 1994 on a plinth re-created after an eighteenth-century engraving.*

Royal residents

Since 1975 the 'private side' of Kensington Palace has continued to fulfil its intended and traditional purpose, as a residence for members of the Royal Family and household staff. New arrivals in this period have included the two sons of George, Duke of Kent and Princess Marina: His Royal Highness Prince Edward, Duke of Kent and His Royal Highness Prince Michael, together with their families. In 1969 Prince Henry, Duke of Gloucester moved to the palace with his family; his heir, Prince Richard, continued to occupy the apartment after his father's death and lives there today with his family and his widowed mother, Princess Alice. The best-known recent residents, however, have undoubtedly been His Royal Highness Charles, Prince of Wales and Diana, Princess of Wales, who moved into the palace in 1984; after their divorce in 1996 the Princess lived on at Kensington, with Princes William and Henry of Wales, until her tragic death in 1997. A major event in the nation's memory, this led to a significant episode in the palace's history as mourners covered thousands of square metres of ground in front of the palace with a sea of flowers and other tributes (fig. 176); over a two-week period, during the first seven days of which the palace was open twenty-four hours a day, over 140,000 people filed through the Red Saloon to sign the books of condolence. For many people in Britain and for most abroad, it is through these moving scenes and memories that the palace is best known.

The State Apartments
Management and administration, 1975–2003
With the withdrawal of the London Museum, care of the State Apartments and (for a while) the rooms beneath was returned to the Government, its responsibilities now discharged by the Department of the Environment (DoE), which in 1970 had absorbed the Ministry of Public Buildings and Works (MPBW), in turn successor to the Ministry of Works in 1969; its work, however, was under the general direction of the Lord Chamberlain's Department. Within the DoE, responsibility for the management and maintenance of

RIGHT 174. *Drawing by Sir Hugh Casson of the entrance to the Prince and Princess of Wales's home at Kensington Palace, presented to the couple by the Royal Institute of British Architects in 1981.*

the State Apartments fell to the Directorate of Ancient Monuments and Historic Buildings (DAMHB) and, after 1972, their maintenance to the Property Services Agency (PSA), successor to the MPBW. Following the passing of the National Heritage Act in 1983, care of most state-controlled Ancient Monuments and Historic Buildings was transferred to the Historic Buildings and Monuments Commission (HBMC), soon to be subtitled English Heritage. The State Apartments at Kensington, however, continued to be maintained by the PSA and managed directly by the DoE, with advice from English Heritage, until, after various interim measures, these functions were taken over by an Executive Agency, the Historic Royal Palaces

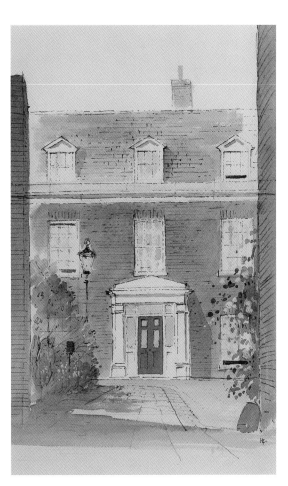

TOP 175. *Diana, Princess of Wales in her dining room at Kensington Palace, her home from 1984 to 1997.*

MIDDLE 176. *The South Front of Kensington Palace in the days following the death of Diana, Princess of Wales, seen across the sea of flowers and other tributes placed there by tens of thousands of mourners.*

BOTTOM 177. *The Princess's funeral cortège leaving Kensington Palace on the morning of 6 September 1997.*

Agency (or HRPA), established in 1989. Along with four other unoccupied royal palaces and buildings no longer used by The Queen – Hampton Court Palace, the Tower of London, Kew Palace and the Banqueting House in Whitehall – Kensington remained in its charge until 1998; in that year HRPA was transformed into a non-Departmental Government Body with charitable status and became entirely dependent on its own business and visitor revenue. Since 1989 HRPA and its successor, Historic Royal Palaces (HRP), have maintained a Curatorial Department responsible for the display of the palaces, the conservation of their contents and advice on the care of the buildings and gardens; within seven years, under the leadership of Simon Thurley and David Beeton, HRPA had pioneered new approaches and techniques in the display of historic buildings, a programme that included major improvements at Kensington (see below). In parallel to this, the care and display of the Royal Collection and the 'occupied' palaces were put on a new administrative and financial footing and given a broader remit, with the foundation of the Royal Collection Trust in 1992.

The display of the State Apartments since 1975
Between 1975 and 1989 the display of the State Apartments remained much as left by the museum, subject to inspections by the Lord Chamberlain, the Surveyor of The Queen's pictures, the Surveyor of The Queen's Works of Art and representatives of DAHMB. The most important improvements of this period were to the King's Gallery, which in the late 1970s was partly redecorated and hung with a selection of paintings similar to that of William III, under the direction of Sir Oliver Millar, Surveyor of The Queen's pictures.

With the establishment of HRPA the pace and scope of improvement could increase. In 1991 a programme was initiated to adjust the decoration and furnishing of the state rooms to reproduce, so far as information and objects permitted, their appearance under William and Mary, under George I and in the time of Princess Victoria. The first rooms to be addressed were those built or decorated (or both) under George I, attention being turned first to the Cupola Room. Here the painted walls and ceiling and the sculptures were cleaned, chandeliers reproducing those made by Gumley and Moore in the 1720s were installed and the extraordinary eighteenth-century clock (fig. 173) was moved there from the King's Drawing Room. Between 1993 and 1995, in a collaborative effort led by Susan Jenkins and the Royal Collection Department, the appearance of the King's Gallery was returned to that of the Kent period, as precisely as the excellent sources, meticulous research and available items would allow: the woodwork was painted in white and gold, the ceiling paintings were conserved and the walls were rehung with specially woven crimson damask and the magnificent selection of pictures there today (fig. 81). The King's Drawing Room received similar, although less extensive, treatment in 1996–97. In 1991 and 1999 temporary displays of porcelain and other Oriental items in the Queen's Gallery (fig. 178) demonstrated the feasibility of redisplaying the Queen's Apartments to evoke their appearance under Mary II. This is one of a wide range of planned and potential improvements that may, dependent on circumstances and resources, be made to the display of the State Apartments, and what they offer to visitors, in the coming years.

The Royal Ceremonial Dress Collection

In the interval between the departure of the London Museum and the establishment of HRPA, Kensington once again became the home of a museum – one not only of national and international significance but also on a subject highly appropriate to its royal status. In the early 1980s a private individual, Aubrey Bowden, offered the long-term loan of his unique collection of court uniforms to Her Majesty The Queen on the understanding that it would be displayed to the

178. *The Queen's Gallery in 1999, furnished with a range of Oriental items of the late seventeenth century, intended to give a flavour of the room's appearance in the time of Mary II.*

public. To the officials who handled the offer, Kensington Palace, with the former museum rooms still empty, seemed an obvious choice, and in anticipation of receiving Bowden's material a curator was appointed, other gifts were received and the museum was established as the Court Dress Collection. Eleven of the former display rooms were redecorated under the direction of Percy Flaxman: the Red Saloon on the basis of historical paint analysis, and the others in colours chosen in keeping with the period of dress to be displayed. Following the departure of the first curator, Valerie Cumming, Nigel Arch was appointed in her place, with Joanna Marschner as Assistant Curator in 1982 and 1983 respectively. The Bowden Collection was then delivered, and the dress collection rapidly grew, its central aim being to represent the history of royal, court and ceremonial dress from the eighteenth century to the present day. On 24 May 1984, the anniversary of Queen Victoria's birth, the newly displayed collection was opened to the public by Princess Margaret, who then took a keen interest in its subsequent development. From then until 1989 the Court Dress Collection staff set up and sustained an education centre and service for schools and mounted a series of exhibitions on both court and royal dress, which included, in 1988, Kensington's contribution to the nationwide commemoration of the Glorious Revolution.

In 1989 responsibility for the Court Dress Collection (soon to be renamed the Royal Ceremonial Dress Collection) was taken over, along with the State Apartments, by HRPA. Since then, in 1996–97, the permanent displays of historic costume have been entirely renewed, and tell, *inter alia*, the story of the creation as well as the wearing of court dress; royal dress is now also an important feature, both in the permanent display – which includes dress on loan from Her Majesty The Queen – and in the temporary

RIGHT 181. *Dresses formerly belonging to Diana, Princess of Wales as displayed at Kensington Palace in 2001–02 in the exhibition* Diana, Princess of Wales: Dresses and Designs by Catherine Walker.

BELOW RIGHT 182. *Staff from the Hampton Court Textile Conservation Studio preparing the wedding dress of Her Majesty The Queen for display in the exhibition* A Century of Queens' Wedding Dresses, *held at Kensington Palace in 2002–03.*

exhibitions programme. It also includes, thanks to the generosity of Ms Rorech Dunkel and The People's Princess Charitable Foundation, Inc, a display of dresses formerly belonging to Diana, Princess of Wales (fig. 181). The temporary exhibition programme, with the collaboration of Jenny Band and the Textile Conservation Studio at Hampton Court Palace, has also been continued: highlights have included *Queen Victoria: Her Life in Dress*, in which her 'accession' dress (figs. 134, 180) was displayed, and *A Century of Queens' Wedding Dresses*, which included that of Her Majesty The Queen (fig. 182).

The presence and activities of the Royal Ceremonial Dress Collection make Kensington (its intrinsic significance as a royal palace and historic monument apart) not only the one museum in the country to represent this theme but also the one that has engaged the public with spectacular success, as evidenced by the 260,000 visitors it played its part in attracting to the palace in 2000–01. At the same time the collection itself, and associated documentation and expertise, has established the museum as an internationally renowned centre of excellence.

FURTHER READING

G.H. Chettle and P.A. Faulkner, 'Kensington Palace and Sir Christopher Wren: A Vindication', *Journal of the British Archaeological Association*, XIV, 1951, pp. 1–10

H. Colvin (ed.), *The History of the King's Works*, London (HMSO) 1973–76, V–VI

T. Faulkner, *History and Antiquities of Kensington*, London 1820

M. Hinton and O. Impey (eds.), *Kensington Palace and the Porcelain of Queen Mary II*, London (Christie's) 1998

Kensington Palace: the Official Guidebook, London (Historic Royal Palaces) 1998

Wren Society, Oxford (Oxford University Press) 1930, VII

INDEX

ACKNOWLEDGEMENTS

The author and publishers would like to thank all those members of the staff of Historic Royal Palaces (HRP) and others who have contributed in any way, large or small, to the preparation of this book. For various combinations and quantities of practical assistance, information and advice on the draft text, particular thanks are due to Nigel Arch, Norma Aubertin-Potter, Barbara Bryant, Mrs Dennis Brangwyn, Toby Cosgrove, Sebastian Edwards, Percy Flaxman, Daphne Ford, Kay Ford, Susanne Groom, Alison Heald, Oliver Impey, Anna Keay, Harry Leslie-Melville, Joanna Marschner, Paul Rem and John Thorneycroft. Many thanks are also due to Annie Heron for assistance in obtaining illustrations, to Back2Front Photography, Paul Highnam and Joshua St John for photography, and to HRP's Publications Manager, Clare Murphy, for managing the picture research, editing the text and much encouragement and patience. Finally, the content of the book owes a great debt to the many scholars who have worked on aspects of Kensington's past and associated people and events, and to the magisterial typescript volumes on the history of the palace prepared by Peter Gaunt and Caroline Knight between 1988 and 1989.

This book is dedicated to the memory of Joan Marjorie Impey (1907–2003).

PICTURE CREDITS

The Family of John Adams of Holyland, Pembrokeshire/ Photograph: Shannon Tofts: fig. 19; The Warden and Fellows of All Souls College, Oxford: figs. 10, 47, 50, 51, 67, 68; Associated Press: fig. 177; Birmingham Library Services: fig. 25; Bomann-Museum Celle: fig. 64; Mrs Dennis Brangwyn: fig. 169; Private Collection/ Bridgeman Art Library: fig. 151; By permission of the British Library: figs. 86 (Add MS 42572c), 95 (61 c 23 plate 3.1); © Copyright The British Museum: figs. 1 (Crace IX 22), 53, 92 (BM Sat 2348), 105 (Crace IX 17), 117 (Crace IX 22); Camera Press Limited: page 5 (second from bottom), fig. 166; A.C. Cooper Ltd: fig. 100; The Country Life Picture Library: fig. 84; By permission of the Trustees of Dulwich Picture Gallery: figs. 119, 131; © English Heritage Photographic Library: fig. 89; © English Heritage GHBAU Photographic Library: fig. 168; Getty Images: fig. 43; Photograph by Tim Graham: page 5 (bottom), fig. 175; Guildhall Library, Corporation of London: figs. 22, 149; His Royal Highness The Prince of Hanover: fig. 65; Paleis Het Loo, The Netherlands: figs. 13, 45; Historic Royal Palaces: inside front cover plan (drawing by Daphne Ford), pages 1, 2, figs. 8, 17, 27, 31, 35, 36, 37, 38, 39, 40, 46, 48, 49, 54, 59, 60, 70, 74, 75, 76, 77, 78, 80, 81, 104, 118, 120, 127, 143, 154, 155, 156, 167, 170, 172, 173, 178, 179, 180, 181, 182, back cover; By permission of the Huntington Library, Art Collections, and Botanical Gardens, San Marino, California, ref ST Map 147: fig. 101; The Illustrated London News Picture Library: figs. 147, 150; Edward Impey: figs. 28, 29, 30; Tim Imrie Tate/ Country Life Picture Library: figs. 72, 73; The Royal Borough of Kensington and Chelsea Libraries and Arts Service: page 5 (middle), figs. 33, 58, 102, 106, 130, 132, 136, 162; London Aerial Photo Library: fig. 56; London Metropolitan Archives: figs. 7, 85; By kind permission of His Grace, the Duke of Marlborough: fig. 55; Mary Evans Picture Library: fig. 148; Courtesy of the Museum of London: figs. 88, 121, 145, 157, 158, 159, 160, 171; Museum of London, UK/ Bridgeman Art Library: fig. 93; By courtesy of the National Portrait Gallery, London: pages 4 (top and bottom), 5 (top), figs. 11, 12, 21, 32, 52, 57, 63, 71, 91, 115, 129, 161; National Trust Photographic Library/ Angelo Hornak: fig. 99; © Crown copyright. NMR: figs. 61, 66, 83, 141, 146, 163; The Pepys Library, Magdalene College, Cambridge: fig. 23; Popperfoto.com: fig. 164; The Public Record Office: figs. 3 (E32/2/2), 26 (Work 5/146), 34 (Work 34/114), 62 (Work 32/312), 69 (Work 6/7 p 69), 87 (Work 32/309), 94 (Work 34/118), 107 (Work 34/118), 125 (Work 34/717), 144 (Work 34/734), 152 (MPE 1/848); Rex Features Limited: figs. 165, 176; Rijksmuseum, Amsterdam: fig. 14; The Royal Archives © 2003 Her Majesty Queen Elizabeth II: figs. 139, 140, 142; The Royal Collection © 2003 Her Majesty Queen Elizabeth II: pages 4 (middle), 5 (second from top), figs. 15, 16, 20, 24, 41, 42, 44, 82, 90, 97, 98, 108, 109, 110, 113, 114, 116, 122, 123, 124, 126, 128, 134, 135, 138, 153; RIBA Library, Drawings Collection: fig. 103; The Trustees of the Sir John Soane's Museum: fig. 9; Society of Antiquaries of London: figs. 4, 5, 6, 111; Picture, Courtesy of Sotheby's Picture Library, London: fig. 79; Joshua St John: front cover; © Tate, London 2002: fig. 133; V & A Picture Library: figs. 96, 112; Reproduced by kind permission of His Royal Highness The Prince of Wales: fig. 174; Westminster City Archives: fig. 18.

Extracts from Queen Victoria's journal are reproduced by permission of Her Majesty The Queen.

HALF-TITLE *Bronze statue of William III by the German sculptor Heinrich Baucke (detail of fig. 156).*

FRONTISPIECE *Preparatory drawing by William Kent for the ceiling of the King's Drawing Room (detail of fig. 74).*

First published 2003 by Merrell Publishers Limited

Head office:
42 Southwark Street
London SE1 1UN

New York office:
49 West 24th Street
New York, NY 10010

www.merrellpublishers.com

in association with

Historic Royal Palaces
Hampton Court Palace
Surrey KT8 9AU

www.hrp.org.uk

Text copyright © 2003 Historic Royal Palaces
Pictures copyright © 2003 the copyright holders; see above for details

British Library Cataloguing-in-Publication data:
Impey, Edward
Kensington Palace : the official illustrated history
1.Kensington Palace – History
I.Title II.Historic Royal Palaces
728.8'2'0942134

ISBN 1 85894 205 5

Edited by Clare Murphy and Laura Hicks
Indexed by Laura Hicks
Designed by Maggi Smith and Stephen Coates

Printed and bound in Singapore